What are you *Doing*?

A conversation about dating and courtship.

There are thousands of Godly young people of both genders who want to get married, are ready to get married, and should be married... indeed they should have been married long ago... who are not married. Their church, their friends, and their families have all prepared them for marriage, for early marriage, for early, fruitful marriage... and they are not married. There is no persecution, no law, no physical infirmities preventing them from being married... but they are not married. This is not a 'panic', it is a crisis.

Worse, we have many of the very best and brightest of our Christian young people, the best taught, from the finest families, and they are already well past the flower of their age; yet they are not married. This is beyond a crisis, it is a catastrophe.

Scripture provides clear answers to this crisis, clear solutions for this catastrophe: solutions we have ignored because they run counter to everything our culture has taught us. It is time we began to take every thought captive to Christ, and throw off the chains of bondage to this world. It is time we 'let them marry'.

We have prepared this document, and our other work on this subject, after long thought, careful study, much prayer, and copious discussion. We covet your feedback.

Von
Von@vonsbooks.com

Also by Vaughn Ohlman

Audio version of What are you *Doing*? in process

Island Peoples Series:

Island Peoples

Come the Day

Dwarves and Dragons (in process)

Available at

www.vonsbooks.com

What are you *Doing*?

Vaughn Ohlman

Acknowledgements

Words cannot express our thanks to the many families, especially of our local fellowship, who have contributed their comments, feedback, and encouragement along the way. Their hours of conversation, discussion and study of the Scriptures with us have truly blessed this work and improved it. Thank you so much.

We would like to acknowledge the guidance of our elders in this work: John Latham, Don Hart, and Jack Youngblood.

Our special thanks to the Nielsen family for their help and encouragement. May the Lord richly bless each of you and use this work for His glory and the edification of His body, the church.

Vaughn Ohlman and family

Table of Characters

Sakal[1] Davidson: A student of the wisdom of Scripture.

Isha[2] Davidson: Sakal's wife, and the mother of his children.

Andrew[3] Adamson: A young man, looking to do God's will.

Abe[4] Adamson: Father of Andrew.

Maydyn[5] Terrefille[6]: An obedient, Godly, young woman.

Pater[7] (Pat) Terrefille: Father of Maydyn.

Beth[8] Terrefille: A Cousin of Maydyn.

Jessie[9] DuMonde[10]: A distant cousin of Maydyn.

Charles Williamson: The youth pastor at Maydyn's church.

George Wakefield: Senior pastor of the local Baptist church.

Andrew: When it does what I want it to do! Which it's not doing now, since it isn't telling me who to call. *[Looking at it ruefully]*

Sakal: So your phone is doing the *wrong* thing by not telling you who to call?

Andrew: No, I was just kidding. The phone wasn't made to tell me who to call, so I can't really blame it.

Sakal: So, doing the right thing means doing what you were made to do?

Andrew: Yeah, I guess so. Isn't that what the Scriptures say? That we were made to obey and glorify our creator, God? How about: *"Wherefore let them that suffer according to the will of God, commit the keeping of their souls to him in well doing, as unto a faithful Creator."*[xiv]

Sakal: So you are suffering according to the will of God?

Andrew: It sure seemed like it when I turned Jessie down! *[Grins]*

Sakal: *[Laughs]* I weep for you.[xv]

Andrew: But, really, I knew I wasn't supposed to get physical with her; I'm supposed to wait until I get married to sleep with a girl. God is pretty clear on that.

Sakal: Good. Back to our main point: you say you want to do the will of God, or the will of your Creator. So, you must ask yourself, what *is* the will of your Creator? What were you made to do?

Andrew: I know *that*! All those years of Sunday school finally pay off: The right thing for me to do is to 'love God and love my neighbor.'[xvi]

Sakal: So that is what you want to do: love God and love your neighbor?

Andrew: Yeah, I guess so.

Sakal: Then our next question would seem to be, *how* do you love God and love your neighbor?

Andrew: We find the answer to that in the Scriptures, in God's word.[xvii]

Sakal: Absolutely, I quite agree. Now that we've determined your primary goal for your life, does that help you decide what your next step should be regarding your date?

Andrew: *[Thinks for a minute]* Yeah, it does. If my goal is to glorify God with my date, then I need to ask a Christian girl out on the date; otherwise I will be trying to do one thing, and she will be trying to do something else.[xviii] Hey, thanks! It's been nice talking to you…

Sakal: But… *[Sakal starts to say, but Andrew has already opened his flip phone and is walking away. Sakal shakes his head, and then, with a small grin turns back to his lunch.]*

II: What should I be doing on a date?

Andrew is sitting at the table picking at his lunch. Sakal comes and sits across from him.

Sakal: How did the date go?

Andrew: *[Looks up, startled]* The date? Oh, that, yes, well, sort of. I mean, we had a good time, went out to a movie and then dinner. But you sort of ruined it for me.

Sakal: *I* did?

Andrew: Yes. Our conversation kept running through my head:[xix] 'loving God', 'loving my neighbor'…

Sakal: Oh? So you were wondering if you should have gone out?

Andrew: No, no but I wasn't sure what I should be *doing* on the date!

Sakal: You mean, going to a movie and dinner or doing something else?

Andrew: No, I mean… *why* was I dating? What was I supposed to be accomplishing on the date? We agreed, last time, that my goal was to love God and love my neighbor. Well, I thought about it a bunch more, and I remembered that part of loving God is glorifying God.

Sakal: *For ye are bought with a price: therefore glorify God in your body, and in your spirit, which are God's.*[xx]

Andrew: Yes, exactly. So I had to ask myself, am I doing that? *How* do I do that? How am I supposed to do that on a date? I'm not sure I did so well on my date.
I took her to see the movie *Titanic*, you know, a romantic movie. Figured it was appropriate for a date. Not my favorite, but girls love it, no? But then I was all embarrassed at the one scene[xxi]… well, a couple of scenes, several scenes, really. I've seen that movie a couple of times before and always enjoyed it. It is only rated PG, but this time, with my mind full of 'glorifying God', it looked very different.
My date didn't seem to object to any of it, and she thanked me for taking her. But the whole time I was watching the movie, and watching my date, I wondered how well I was doing at the whole 'glorifying God' thing? How am I supposed to do that on my dates?

Sakal: You know you are supposed to glorify God while dating, but you don't know how that is to be accomplished on a date, or by dating?

Andrew: Yes, exactly! It isn't enough to know I am supposed to glorify God with my life if I can't figure out how to do so with this activity. I'm supposed to glorify God with *all* of my life right, not just parts of it?[xxii]

Sakal: An excellent principle. So what do the Scriptures say about dating? Perhaps you should study that.

Andrew: They don't say *anything* about dating! How could they? They didn't 'date' back then. They just, I don't know *what* they did, but they didn't date. But we date nowadays, so I have to figure out how to do it right.

Sakal: But...

Andrew: Look, it's what you said the other day... your rule. I had to try to do what my goal was, because I am human... so, what should be my goal for this activity? What about what I was created to do can I do on my dates?

Sakal: Well, let me ask you this; is dating a means to an end, or an end in itself? The other day you said you wanted the date itself to be 'fun', and to be 'right', which sounds like you want to date for the sake of dating. Is that true, or is a date a means to some other end?

Andrew: Well of course. You don't date just to date... *I* don't anyway. But even if I am dating for an eventual purpose, I still need to glorify God while I am actually on a date, no?

Sakal: Quite right, you need to do both: glorify God *during* the date, *and* by the purpose of the date. But let us examine that eventual purpose. Why do you date? What end does it serve?

Andrew: To get married, of course. I want to get married, eventually, and everyone knows you can't get married without dating...

Sakal: Do they? I don't seem to know that. I thought you said the people back when the Scriptures were written didn't date. Did they not get married?

Andrew: Oh, them. I mean nowadays. You can't get married *nowadays* without dating.

Sakal: But... well, perhaps another day. So you wish to date, in order to get married. And you wish to get married... why?

Andrew: Well, there are lots of reasons... companionship, kids...

Sakal: And are those the only reasons?

Andrew: *[Blushing]* Well, and, you know...

Sakal: The physical aspect?

Andrew: *[Nods]*

Sakal: You are looking forward to that part?

Andrew: *[Blushing even brighter, and looking around in hopes no one is overhearing this, nods again.]*

Sakal: One wonders what this world is coming to that a young man is embarrassed to admit he wants to get married because he wants to sleep with his wife. Everyone knows it, but no one is willing to say it. So companionship, children, rejoicing in each other physically ... is that it?

Andrew: And to glorify God! I mean, all of that is supposed to glorify God. There are two ways I could glorify God with my life right now. I could stay unmarried, or I could get married. I could seek a wife, or I could ignore girls.

Sakal: Oh?

Andrew: Yes. Except I *can't* ignore girls.[xxiii] I don't think I have it in me. So I think I should get married and have a wife, if you see what I mean.

Sakal: I do indeed. Once you get married, will it then glorify God for you to sleep with each other? As opposed to what Jessie wanted you to do?

Andrew: Well, yes. I mean, that is what the Scriptures say, several of them.[xxiv] It seems wild to me, but I'm perfectly willing to trust God on *that!*[xxv]

Sakal: So you want to date in order to get married, and you want to get married in order to have sex, and you want to have sex because it will glorify God?

Andrew: Yes, I mean... no, I mean...*[He lowers his voice]* I want to have sex; God made me to want to have sex, and he says that sex in marriage *does* glorify Him. And a lot of other things in marriage, too.[xxvi] *All* of marriage is supposed to glorify God: having kids,[xxvii] raising a family in the Lord[xxviii], *all* those things.

Sakal: So, marriage is a good thing... or at least the *results* of marriage. Do you see marriage by itself as being a good thing?

Andrew: Yes, oh, yes. As a matter of fact our pastor preached on that the other day. In Ephesians five we learned that our marriages are supposed to be a reflection of the marriage of Christ and the church. That because Christ is one with His Church, we should become one with our wife[xxix]. Pastor said our human marriages, not just the marriage of Christ but our earthly, human, marriages, are a witness to the gospel. That by getting married, staying married, and having a Godly marriage where we love each other and all that, we can show people what being a Christian is supposed to be all about, at least part of it.

Sakal: Ok, so there are a lot of reasons to want to get married.

Andrew: Yes... and it tells me who I ought to be dating! I never thought this out before, not really, not like this.

Sakal: Oh?

Andrew: Yes! If I am supposed to be dating in order to get married, then I should be dating a girl I would be actually willing to marry, not just any Christian girl. And, of all the girls in my 'black book', the only one I can really see myself marrying is my friend Maydyn, Maydyn Terrefille. What an idiot I've been! *[He picks up his phone and starts dialing as he walks off...]*

Sakal: But...? *[Sighs and walks away.]*

III: The Importance of Boyfriends.

Sakal and Andrew are sitting at a table in the park, just opening their lunches when a girl walks up.

Jessie: Hey, you!

Andrew: Jessie?

Jessie: Yeah, Jessie. So you remember me? *[Sarcastically]*

Andrew: Of course, Jessie. *[Looking confused]* Jessie, this is Mr. Davidson, a friend of mine. Mr. Davidson, this is Jessie Dumonde...

Jessie: His girlfriend, or so I thought! How come you didn't call me this weekend? I had to spend Friday night catching up on laundry and homework, and if there is anything I hate more than doing laundry on Friday night, it's doing homework.

Sakal: So you expected Andrew to call you?

Jessie: Yes!

Sakal: For a date?

Jessie: Yes!

Sakal: Had he *told* you he would call you?

Jessie: No. But when a guy takes a girl out a couple of times in a row, and they get all *interested* in each other, then she expects he will call again, no?

Sakal: I did *not* know. So, dating, at least if you date 'a couple of times' and 'you get all interested in each other', implies obligations.

Jessie: Say, Andrew, who is this guy, anyway? He asks weird questions.

Andrew: He's a friend of mine, and he knows a lot of Scripture, and we've been talking about dating.

Jessie: You are going to date *him*?! *[She leers at Andrew]* No wonder…

Andrew: No!! *[Blushing]* I meant we were talking *about* dating. He's not from here and doesn't know about dating…

Jessie: Oh, like from overseas. Cool! You do look kind of foreign. So what do you want to know about dating?

Sakal: Well, the first question I had was, why date at all?

Jessie: For the relationship! No one wants to be alone, like I was on Friday night.

Sakal: So, for you, the *relationship* is the goal?

Jessie: Yeah, no girl wants to be the only one without a boyfriend.

Sakal: A 'boyfriend'?

Jessie: Yeah, that's what you call a boy you go on dates with.

Sakal: I see. And what do you want out of a boyfriend?

Jessie: Well, at first you just want the dates. But then, once you've gotten to know each other, you want to be together a lot.

Sakal: Does it matter what you do together?

Jessie: Nah. I mean, different couples like to do different things. One couple I know likes doing homework together. I can't see it myself but, whatever floats their boat. Mostly you just do stuff together, and have someone to talk about with the other girls.

Sakal: Is that important, talking about it with your girlfriends?

Jessie: Oh, yes! That's *very* important.

Sakal: Would you say you feel like less of a person, if you don't have a boyfriend?

Jessie: Wow. That's deep. But yeah, I think you're right.

Sakal: And that makes it important to have a boyfriend? So you can be who you want to be, in the eyes of everyone around you?

Jessie: Yes.

Sakal: Is that why you wanted to sleep with Andrew?

Andrew: Mr. Davidson!

Jessie: Andrew?! You told him?

Sakal: Are you embarrassed he told me? Was it a secret you wanted to sleep with him?

Jessie: Well, no, not really. I was more surprised you would tell me you two had talked about it. I hear most guys boast about their sex life, but I didn't know they talked about *not* getting it! Did he tell you why he didn't want to?

Sakal: Yes. Because he wasn't sure it was right.

Andrew: Actually, I was pretty sure it wasn't. I mean, I *know* it wasn't.

Sakal: *[Turning back to Andrew]* But you were tempted to think it was OK?

Andrew: *[Nods glumly]*

Jessie: What's wrong with us sleeping together? It isn't like Andrew and I had just met! We'd been going out for quite a while.

Sakal: If you don't mind, I would rather not get into that just yet.[xxx] I was interested in your reasons for dating, which seemed different from Andrew's. I am also interested in your reasons for wanting to sleep together, which also seem different from his.

Jessie: What are his reasons?

Sakal: Well, one reason is because he imagines it would feel good.

Jessie: That's my reason, too. *[Grins]*

Sakal: Is it? So you want to date for the relationship, but you just want to have sex because it's fun?

Jessie: Yeah, sure!

Sakal: And that's it? Sex, fun, then move on to somebody else?

Jessie: No! What do you take me for?

Sakal: So, the relationship is still important?

Jessie: Of course. Sex is fun, but it is really the relationship that is important for the girl. Let's face it, nowadays everybody knows if you don't put out the guy won't like it and then he'll drop you.

Sakal: I had thought that might be part of the reason. So when Andrew turned you down for sex, and then when he didn't call you for a date the next week…

Jessie: I got the picture! He didn't want *me* anymore. But it would have been nice of him to have told me!

Andrew: I'm sorry, I had no idea…

Jessie: What do you mean you had no idea?! Why did you think I wanted to sleep with you?

Andrew: I thought, I thought we were just having fun together. I didn't know it meant all *that* to you!

Jessie: Well, it did! *[Walks off angrily]*

Andrew: *[Looks helplessly at Sakal]* What did I do? How could I have been so stupid?

Sakal: *He shall die without instruction; and in the greatness of his folly he shall go astray.*[xxxi]

Andrew: What?

Sakal: Perhaps you need to examine not just your goals, but the other person's goals, when you begin a relationship. It seems when Jessie accepted your invitation to 'date', she heard more than you thought you were saying. She had hopes that your request to date was the first step toward something much more serious: in her eyes, a 'relationship'. You, on the other hand, were just looking to 'have fun'.
You not only 'took her out' once, but several times, and her expectations grew, until she felt secure in calling you her 'boyfriend', at least to herself. Then, when you decided to move on to someone else, that relationship was destroyed, and she was hurt.
If I understand the situation correctly, because you have rejected her, she is also now shamed in the eyes of her girlfriends. She has been, I believe the word is, 'dumped'.

Andrew: So, from now on, she will always feel 'rejected' by me. We will have a broken relationship, not just a non-dating relationship.

Sakal: And that is probably not her first time. She may have given part of her heart to a dozen boys already, and will give it to yet a dozen more.

Andrew: The poor boy at the end…!

Sakal: What?

Andrew: He will have to compete with the memory of all of those others![xxxii]

Sakal: A wise observation.

IV: Courting a distinction.

Sakal comes to the table and sees Andrew and a girl arguing.

Sakal: What's wrong?

Andrew: Oh, Hi! Maydyn, this is Mr. Davidson, the guy I was telling you about. And Mr. Davidson, this is Maydyn Terrefille, the girl I was telling *you* about. *[Sakal and Maydyn shake hands]*
You remember how we agreed that I should only go on a date with someone I might want to marry? Well, I called Maydyn and told her all about it. She thought it was a good idea, and said I was a nice boy and all, but that she couldn't date me because she won't date at all!

Maydyn: I didn't say that, or not like that, you know I didn't. I said that in *my* family, we don't date, we court.

Andrew: Anyway, I got upset and thought she meant she just wouldn't date *me*. But then she came up to me today and said it wasn't that, but that she believes in 'courtship', which I don't understand at all.
You know the Bible well, you proved that to me the other day... what is this 'courtship' she's trying to tell me about? And what does the Bible teach about it?

Sakal: Well, I can't really say. The word 'courtship' isn't in the Bible, so there is no help there. Perhaps if Maydyn told me what she means by the word, we could explore it together.

Maydyn: Well, it's kind of old fashioned. That's probably why you haven't heard about it.

Sakal: I didn't say I hadn't heard of it. But as you may know, there are as many definitions of courtship as there are advocates of courtship. The only way to tell anything about a given form of courtship, or how Biblical it is, is to find out exactly what the person means by 'courtship'.

Maydyn: Well, you can find one definition on Bill Gothard's website. Have you heard of Bill Gothard?

Sakal: Oh, yes. Even where I come from we have heard of Bill Gothard.

Maydyn: Well, we certainly don't agree with everything he teaches, but he is very popular, and was at the forefront of the courtship movement. His definition goes like this: *"Courtship is experiencing the blessing of God by loving the Lord Jesus Christ and honoring both sets of parents. The purpose of courtship is to determine a couple's readiness for marriage and to discern the will of God for a covenant marriage that will benefit the world."*

Sakal: And?

Maydyn: And what?

Sakal: I thought from what Andrew said that you didn't believe in dating.

Maydyn: I don't, we don't.

Sakal: But nothing in your definition spoke to that; to the differences between dating and courting.

Maydyn: Oh, well, you see, courting means you don't date.

Sakal: But why? How are they different? How do you know when you are doing one and not the other?

Maydyn: Well, first of all, dating is just for fun, and courting is serious.

Andrew: But I told you I didn't want to date you 'just for fun'! I told you I *was* serious! I told her all this, Mr. Davidson!

Maydyn: Yes, but you asked me out on a 'date', and I don't 'date', I *court*.

Sakal: Which we have not yet defined. Andrew, here, asked you out on a date, and was serious, so the 'serious' issue cannot separate dating from courting... at least not in this case.

Maydyn: Well, yes, I suppose, if you look at it like that. But there are lots of other differences.

Sakal: So let us explore again: what are the difference between dating and courting?

Maydyn: There are lots of differences! They are *completely* different.

Sakal: Perhaps, but so far we haven't found any. Andrew was serious with his request for a date, so by your definition, it seems he was trying to 'court' you.

Maydyn: No, no. Maybe you should put it this way; in dating, only some people are serious, most are out to have fun. In courting, everyone is serious.

Sakal: So courting is a kind of dating? A kind of dating where everyone is serious?

Maydyn: No, I told you, they are completely different.

Sakal: Well, let's keep looking for a difference then. When Andrew came to you and asked you for a date, was it the word itself which led you to refuse? Should he have said, 'a court'?

Maydyn: No! *[Laughs]* I've never heard anyone say *that* before, but I think you have found an important difference. You see, there is no 'a' court. Courting is an entire process, a serious process. He would have asked for 'permission to court' me. You remember the definition I told you before. Courting is meant to: *"determine a couple's readiness for marriage and to discern the will of God for a covenant marriage that will benefit the world."*[xxxiii] That's the reason for the whole system.

Andrew: But that's what I wanted to do! Ask Mr. Davidson yourself! That was why I asked you out! I decided that my purpose for dating was to get married, and in order to do that, I needed to date someone I could be serious about. And of all the girls I know, you are the only person I can see marrying.

Maydyn: *[Blushing furiously]* Well, thank you for the compliment. But we can't do that by *dating*!

Sakal: Really? No couples have ever married after dating?

Maydyn: Of course they have, my own parents did. We just learned about courting a few years ago. Pretty much everyone in my parent's generation got married by dating, courting is so new.

Sakal: Were they ready to get married, your parents?

Maydyn: Well, I *think* they were. My Dad was twenty-seven and already had a good job, and my Mom was twenty-four and was a nurse.

Sakal: And does that mean they were ready?

Maydyn: I guess so... At least, they must have thought they were.

Sakal: How did they determine if they were ready? Was it by courting or by dating?

Maydyn: Well, they didn't court, like I told you; so I guess they figured it out while dating.

Sakal: Well then, that doesn't seem to be the difference. Perhaps it is this question of a 'covenant marriage'. Perhaps couples that date don't arrive at a 'covenant marriage'. Do your parents have some other kind of marriage?

Maydyn: Of course not! They are *Christians*! They were married in church and everything.

Sakal: And a covenant marriage is one that happens in church?

Maydyn: It can't happen anywhere else. Surely you know that!

Sakal: I don't seem to know that. As Andrew was telling you, I tend to know things that are in God's Word, and none of the marriages in Scripture were held in a church building.

Maydyn: Well, not in *Bible* times!

Sakal: So, covenant marriages happened some other way in Bible times?

Maydyn: Of course!

Sakal: Well, then, your definition still doesn't separate courting from dating. Those who date can do so seriously, which was your first point; they can determine if they are ready for marriage; which was in your definition of courting; and they can arrive at a covenant marriage; which was also in the definition. They can do so as an entire 'process' as well. So what do we have left?

Maydyn: The parents. You remember the part about involving the parents in the process?

Sakal: Oh. So you would invite your parents along on the date?

Maydyn: It's not a *date*! And no, we are not *that* conservative! Some people do that, all chaperoned and everything, but *we* don't, or, we *wouldn't*, I haven't actually courted yet. No, the parents *oversee* the process.

Sakal: But not by coming along on the date? So what *do* they do?

Maydyn: Well, first of all, they are involved at the beginning. The young man has to go to the girl's father...

Sakal: And ask if he can date his daughter?

Maydyn: It's not *dating*! He asks for permission to court her.

Sakal: Is that what makes it courting? That he asks the father?

Maydyn: Yes! That and the other things we talked about.

Sakal: So, let me see if I understand... A young man goes to a girl's father, and asks her out on a serious date, or, a series of dates, all part of a process of exploring together whether or not they are ready for a covenant marriage?

Maydyn: It's not a *date*! That would just be dating! Or, Christian dating, or something...

Sakal: I don't understand. I seem to have followed your definition perfectly: the boy asked the father, he was serious, they were exploring readiness for a covenant marriage; it was a process...

Maydyn: But they weren't glorifying God! That was the most important part of our definition, and the part you are leaving out. Courting is glorifying to God.

Andrew: But that is what I want to do. I may not be good at it, I'll grant you, but that's what I wanted to do.

Maydyn: You can't do it by *dating*.

Sakal: But why not? What is it about courting as opposed to dating, that makes it glorifying to God? Surely it can't be the word; the word 'court' doesn't appear in Scripture.

Maydyn: No, but all the principles do!

Sakal: Oh? Where? Which one?

Maydyn: Are you kidding?

Sakal: Not at all. I know the Scriptures rather well and, except for glorifying God and covenant marriage, nothing you have said is in Scripture that I have ever seen. And you admitted that people who don't 'court' can also arrive at a covenant marriage, so that doesn't help. As for glorifying God, you haven't shown how courtship does that and dating doesn't.
Indeed, every time we go back to the Scriptures, we find people weren't doing what you say they should do, and yet you insist that they, or at least some of them, were still doing the right thing.

Maydyn: But, that's crazy. Scripture is filled with these principles!

Sakal: Where?

Maydyn: Everywhere. All of the marriages. None of them dated!

Sakal: True. But none of them *courted* either.

Maydyn: Of course not, it wasn't their culture.

Sakal: So none of those marriages glorified God?

Maydyn: Of course they did! There are some wonderful stories of marriages in Scripture! Rebecca, Ruth, Esther, even Eve. Not to say those people were perfect of course, but God gave us those marriages as examples to learn from.

Sakal: And they glorified God?

Maydyn: Of course! Peter even uses them as examples for how we should behave as wives.

Sakal: So they got married, without courting, and yet they glorified God? So they just started glorifying God *after* they were married... since they got married in such a 'bad' way.

Maydyn: I didn't say it was a *bad* way.

Sakal: But you said only courtship glorifies God... that was how we were to separate it from dating. And yet now you say all of those 'old fashioned' marriages also glorified God.

Maydyn: You just don't understand!

Sakal: No, I don't.

Andrew: So, Mr. Davidson, you are saying that *dating* is better? More Biblical?

Sakal: No, so far I haven't seen any evidence that either one is Biblical.

Maydyn: What?! I don't know where you found this guy, Andrew, but he is crazy! *[Maydyn storms off in a swirl of skirts]*.

Andrew: Wow. That was interesting. But now what should I do? *[Looks at his phone]* Say, I have to go, but will you be here tomorrow? I have lots more questions.

Sakal: Sure...

V: A Return to Courting.

Andrew: Hey, glad you could come.

Sakal: I'm glad you are eager to talk. I often feel I am just shouting out to a city, and everyone is passing me by.[xxxiv]

Andrew: *[Chuckles]*

Sakal: So what is our subject for today?

Andrew: I would like to talk about dating, if you don't mind. After our last conversation with Maydyn, I kept thinking about dating, and whether or not I should date or 'court' instead. Maydyn didn't explain herself very well, but it seemed like part of what she was saying was what we were saying that first day: that we shouldn't date just for fun. But my mind kept going back to the Scriptures...[xxxv]

Sakal: A good place for it to go.

Andrew: Yeah. And when I thought about the Scriptures, well, it seems to me that God *does* want us to have fun[xxxvi]. He keeps talking about being 'blessed' and 'joyful'...even happy. Those are all 'fun' words, no?

Sakal: Certainly... although it might be better to say 'fun' was a 'joyful' word, but I certainly see what you mean. We don't worship a frowning, somber God, but a God who rejoices with us. You recall our conversations about marriage. God once said, about a wife... *"How fair and how pleasant art thou, O love, for delights! This thy stature is like to a palm tree, and thy breasts to clusters of grapes. I said, I will go up to the palm tree, I will take hold of the boughs thereof: now also thy breasts shall be as clusters of the vine, and the smell of thy nose like apples; And the roof of thy mouth like the best wine for my beloved, that goeth down sweetly, causing the lips of those that are asleep to speak".*[xxxvii]

Andrew: If you keep talking like that, you are going to drive me *crazy!*

Sakal: Oh, you don't enjoy the subject?

Andrew: I enjoy it *all* too well! Except there is nothing I can do about it!

Sakal: Oh?

Andrew: *[Looks at him, shocked]* Surely you aren't suggesting I should just go and sleep with a girl? I thought we covered that?

Sakal: No, far from it. Is it not written, *"To keep thee from the evil woman, from the flattery of the tongue of a strange woman. Lust not after her beauty in thine heart; neither let her take thee with her eyelids"?*[xxxviii] If your goal is to do the right thing, the thing that glorifies God, then you need to be joined in one flesh to your wife and her alone, not some strange woman.

Andrew: Well, then, I can't sleep with any girl!

Sakal: And why not?

Andrew: Because I don't have a wife!

Sakal: Well, get one.

Andrew: I can't get one without dating, and I can't figure out what I am supposed to do on a date...

Sakal: But...

Andrew: *[Interrupting]* No. Listen! We agreed the Scriptures are no help for what to do on a date, because no one in Scripture dated. So that throws us back on our own resources, our own wisdom. You seem like a pretty wise guy, so I decided to ask you again what you think... I mean, I was thinking back to my situation with Jessie. She and I 'went out', which meant we went somewhere together, just the two of us. I'm a Christian, and you know I want to be physically pure... well, I want to want to anyway; it's quite a battle. But it's hard when just the two of us go somewhere. She has her own room at college, well she shares it with a roommate, but her roommate, disappears whenever we show up. So there we are, alone, in her bedroom! With a locked door and...

Sakal: ...which is a great temptation for you. As it is written: ***"And beheld among the simple ones, I discerned among the youths, a young man void of understanding, passing through the street near her corner; and he went the way to her house, in the twilight, in the evening, in the black and dark night".***[xxxix]

Andrew: Yes!

Sakal: So, do you think my wife and I ought never to be alone, in her bedroom, behind a locked door?

Andrew: *[Blushing furiously]* No! I mean yes. I mean, you ought to be...

Sakal: Oh? So what is the difference?

Andrew: You two are married! It's what you are supposed to do. I mean, married people... *[Suddenly Andrew notices Maydyn walking up to the table, looking awkward but determined. The two men get up.]* Oh, Hi Maydyn!

Maydyn: Hello. May I sit down? *[Sakal and Andrew wave graciously to a spare seat]* Thank you. I wanted to apologize for yesterday, for walking away like that. I had a long talk with my father last night, and he really helped me understand more of what we should look for in the Scripture here.

Sakal: Well, Andrew, perhaps here is some of that wisdom you were looking for. What did your father say, Maydyn?

Maydyn: He said maybe we were looking for too much in Scripture. He said that Scripture is fine for salvation, and running the church and everything, but it doesn't tell us how to live our lives step by step. We can't use it to build a mousetrap, for example.

Andrew: That can't be right...![xl] *[Sakal holds up his hand, and Andrew subsides, sputtering.]*

Sakal: If that is true, then when you say the courtship system is 'God honoring' what do you mean, since you can't mean that it is what Scripture *specifically* tells you to do?

Maydyn: I'm saying that it uses Godly principles that we find in Scripture, where they aren't talking specifically about courtship, and applies them *to* courtship. So, for example, God teaches against fornication.[xli] Everyone who dates fornicates...

Andrew: *[Interrupting]* Hey!

Maydyn: *[Embarrassed]* Well, maybe not everyone, not... all the way. But there is a lot of physical involvement, and that is basically fornication, isn't it? Should you be kissing someone who will be someone else's wife? Do you want a wife someone else has been kissing? *[Andrew, after a moment's thought, shakes his head.]*

Sakal: It is written, *"I have made a covenant with my eyes, why then should I think upon a maid?"*[xlii]

Andrew: What?

Maydyn: Huh?

Sakal: Just something I thought applied...
So, do you see the idea of physical purity, no physical involvement before marriage, as another distinction between courtship and dating?

Maydyn: Well, yes.

Andrew: *[With a glance at Sakal]* So then, if a boy came to your father, and said he wanted to date you seriously, as part of an entire system, with a view toward a covenant marriage. And if he promised there would be no physical involvement until you two were married... could he take you out on a date?

Maydyn: I don't... I mean... that would be courting... I think... if Father approved...

Andrew: *[Grins]* So, what's your father's phone number at work?

Maydyn: I... I... 555-1212[xliii] *[She blushes and looks at the ground, and then walks away, looking very confused.]*

Andrew: *[Grins]* Well, I may just have a date for Friday night after all. *[He opens up his flip phone and starts typing]*

Sakal: But...?

VI: When am I ready?

Isha Davidson, Sakal's wife, is walking through the park and sees Maydyn sitting on a bench, looking very upset

Isha: You look like you need a hug.

Maydyn: *[The girls hug, Maydyn looking awkward]* Do I know you?

Isha: No, but *I* know of you. My husband, Sakal Davidson, told me about the conversations you and Andrew have been having with him. Did you have a bad 'date'? *[She grins]*

Maydyn: Bad? We didn't have one at all. My dad said, "No".

Isha: Oh, I'm so sorry.

Maydyn: You are? I thought you would be ready with the same lecture.

Isha: Lecture?

Maydyn: My dad's lecture... about how neither of us are ready for marriage, and how we need to wait more on the Lord's will.

Isha: So when Andrew called, your Father just said, "no", right away, without any explanation?

Maydyn: Oh, no. He said he would pray about it. And then when I got home he grilled me about Andrew, and how it was that he had asked, and everything, our whole conversation. We kept praying about it and waiting on the Lord all week, then, Friday, a couple of hours before Andrew was to come by... my dad, of course, hadn't called him back, so he had no idea if he could come by or not... Dad finally decided that it didn't feel right: because Andrew was too immature, and couldn't truly be a Godly young man if he kept talking about 'going on a date'.
So he called Andrew and told him, and then he came and lectured me. He told me how I was still too immature and not ready for marriage. The way he talked, I'll never be ready. I mean, I *am* an adult!

Isha: Are you?

Maydyn: Sure, I turned eighteen last month.

Isha: So that makes you an adult?

Maydyn: Well, legally.

Isha: …and in the eyes of God?

Maydyn: I… I don't know. I don't think… I don't remember anything about becoming an adult in the Scriptures. That's funny. But it does say 'woman', that must be the same thing.

Isha: Must it?

Maydyn: Oh, you are just like your husband!

Isha: *[Laughs]* Thank you.

Maydyn: Can't you just tell me? What is the definition of adult in the Scriptures?

Isha: There isn't one. The Scriptures talk about children, and then men and women, but the word, or the idea of 'adult' as we use it nowadays, never shows up in Scripture.

Maydyn: But… so … when…?

Isha: When what?

Maydyn: When am I ready for marriage? Why does my dad think I'm not?

Isha: Well, I can't tell you what your dad thinks, but as far as Scripture is concerned, you are ready.

Maydyn: Really? How do you know? We just met!

Isha: Well, you see, the only qualification Scripture implies for a woman is…[xliv] *[Isha leans forward and whispers into Maydyn's ear, who blushes]*

Maydyn: *[Blushing brightly]* Really? Where does it say that?

Isha: In the Song of Songs… in what you would call Chapter 8: verses 8-10 and in Ezekiel 16:7-8.

Maydyn: But, that's silly! How can that be all that is needed? Don't you know all the things a wife has to be…? Oh *[She blushes]* of course you do… you've been married…?

Isha: Twenty-years, and we have eight children.

Maydyn: Eight? Wow… so you must know what it takes! You aren't saying that once, you know, you have to get married?

Isha: No, no. I'm saying the opposite: that you shouldn't get married until you are 'grown'. But I am also saying that when we look at Scripture, we don't find lists of 'all the things that you need to do before you get married.' Instead, all of the reasons listed for marriage are designed for the youth; Scripture speaks of marriage 'in youth'[xlv]. It doesn't talk, at all, about multiple forms of maturity or readiness, but of marrying young, and blessing your husband for as long as you both shall live.

Maydyn: But... wow, I had never thought about it that way. So my father is wrong?

Isha: I am not here to tell you your father is wrong, *he* is your father after all.

Maydyn: But you said he wasn't my father anymore. I mean, you said I was an adult now... a woman at least... so I should be making my own decisions, shouldn't I?

Isha: Oh? Where do you read that?

Maydyn: It says '*children* obey your parents'.[xlvi]

Isha: And you aren't a child anymore, so you should disobey your parents?

Maydyn: Not 'disobey'... but I don't really have to 'obey' them anymore, do I? Just honor them.

Isha: I think you will find that it says 'children obey' and 'children honor', if you read it carefully.[xlvii]. And the word 'children' is not the kind of word you are thinking about... it doesn't mean 'little, immature person', it means 'offspring of', and it implies lifelong obedience[xlviii].

Maydyn: Even when it comes to who I may or may not court? I know I believe in courtship and all, and I do really want to glorify God with my path to marriage, but I still have a hard time thinking about Dad just *telling me* that Andrew can't court me.

Isha: You want to chose someone yourself?

Maydyn: Of course... I mean... I think so. I've known Andrew pretty much my entire life, but it is still scary to think about marrying him; or even courting him.

Isha: Yes, it *is* scary. I'm sure your dad is scared.

Maydyn: My dad?

Isha: Sure. Let's say he lets some guy court you, or marry you... and then it 'doesn't work out'... how do you suppose he will feel?

Maydyn: You think that is why he said Andrew couldn't court me?

Isha: That is probably part of it. It's a big, scary, responsibility.

Maydyn: I never thought of that. *[She looks at her phone]* I have to go now, thanks so much for talking to me.

Isha: You're welcome. Let's talk again sometime.

[They hug, again, and Maydyn walks off]

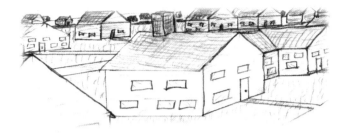

VII: Courting Delays.

Maydyn: There she is! Mrs. Davidson, I'm so glad to see you! I was hoping I would. This is Beth, Beth[xlix] Terrefille, my cousin.

Isha: Hello Beth. So, Maydyn, you were hoping to see me?

Maydyn: Yes. I was hoping you and Beth could talk. She's my cousin, and has experience with courtship and I was hoping she could explain it better than I did. I told her you were interested in courtship.

Isha: Why, yes. My husband and I have been making quite a little study out of it. You say you have courted?

Beth: Yes. My family read *'Her Hand in Marriage'* by Douglas Wilson.[l] It is a wonderful book, you should read it. It tells all about how to get married in the Biblical way.

Isha: Yes, we have read it.

Beth: Oh, then you know. It is so wonderful, and so Biblical.

Isha: Really? We went through it several times, and we found almost nothing 'Biblical' about it.

Beth: What? Why, it was a wonderful exposition!

Isha: But an exposition of what? He does not provide a single example from anywhere in Scripture of anything he talks about.

Beth: He mentions lots of Scriptural examples: Abraham and Sarah, Isaac and Rebecca, Jacob and Rachel…[li]

Isha: True, but he doesn't provide any of them as examples of courtship.[lii]

Beth: Of course not, none of them courted!

Isha: Which is our point, or part of it at least. But, I'm certainly glad it worked for you. How long have you been married?

Beth: Oh, I'm not married, not yet.

Isha: You're still courting?

Beth: No, not right now.

Isha: But I thought you said...

Beth: Not all courtships lead to marriage, you know.

Isha: I had hoped... so your courtship didn't work out?

Beth: I had two, actually.

Isha: And what happened?

Beth: Well, the first one was when I was eighteen. I was so excited. My father came to me and said this twenty-two year old man was interested in courting me.
He was a wonderful young man, an evangelist. He was a cartoonist, and he would go to church meetings, ball games, and the like, and he would draw these wonderful cartoons talking about Biblical characters, or God's love... that kind of thing.

Isha: And what happened?

Beth: Well, we wrote back and forth for a while, he lived out of state, and then my dad broke it off. He said the young man didn't have a good enough job, he wasn't college educated, and he didn't have a good enough financial basis to be thinking about marriage.

Isha: But, I don't understand. You are saying that he allowed a young man to court you who didn't have a 'good job', wasn't 'college educated', and didn't 'have a good enough financial basis to be thinking about marriage' but then, after you had courted a while, when you were getting close to being engaged, he broke off the relationship for those reasons?!

Beth: Yes, yes. And, I must say, some of the young man's friends were rather upset at my father. They said if he had wanted to object about that he shouldn't have let the courtship go on at all.

Isha: What is he doing now?

Beth: Oh, about the same. He supports himself and his ministry with odd jobs.

Isha: He isn't married?

Beth: No.

Isha: And how do you feel about not having married him?

Beth: I, umm, well. I know I shouldn't, but I often think about him... what it would have been like to have been married to him.

Isha: *[After a pause]* What of your second courtship?

Beth: That was three years ago. A very nice young man from a sister church asked my father if we could court. We courted for six months before he, the young man, broke it off.

Isha: What was the problem?

Beth: He decided that we weren't 'like-minded' enough. I remember the night when he told me. He actually quoted from Doug Wilson's book, or paraphrased anyway: "It isn't enough that we both would go to heaven if we died, the Bible requires us only to court those who are like minded." Oh, how I cried.
But he said it would never work: I believe that infants should be baptized, and that someone can't lose their salvation… and he didn't agree with those doctrines.
He was right of course; who knows what would have happened if we had married?

Isha: God.

Beth: What?

Isha: God knows. Perhaps, after a couple of years you would have realized that only believers should be baptized, and he would have realized salvation is in the hands of a God who never lets go. Or, perhaps not. God knows.
So, two failed courtships? I'm so sorry for you.

Beth: *[Breezily]* Oh, we don't call them failed courtships.[liii] That's part of the whole courtship process, you know, part of making sure the eventual marriage really is in the Lord's will.

Isha: Oh? If you don't mind my asking, how old are you?

Beth: *[After a pause]* I'm thirty-two.

Isha: And you don't think a system that has left you unmarried and barren at thirty-two has failed?

Beth: *[Shocked]* I… I'm still hoping… *[Bursts into tears]*

Isha: I'm sure you are dear, *[Hugs her]* and I'm sorry for you.

Beth: *[Dries her tears]* Do you, do you still want to hear about courtship?

Isha: More than you've already told me?

Beth: But I haven't told you hardly anything.

Isha: You've shown me that courtship is a system which calls being a thirty-two year old woman barren and unmarried a 'success'. Are there many other girls like you?

Beth: Oh, yes. Not many quite as old as I am, but lots of girls are unmarried.[liv]

Isha: And all practice courtship?

Beth: Mostly. We are very conservative.

Isha: And do they believe in marriage? In families?

Beth: Oh, yes, and we love children! I love children…

Maydyn: *[After sitting in silence for a few minutes]* I never really thought about it that way but *[She glanced at Beth]* if we want a husband, and children, and we go into a courtship… it must, at least, *feel* like a failure if we don't get married.[iv]

Beth: It did to me. I cried for days the second time. It's funny. I always felt I was such a failure for thinking of my courtships as failures; like being disappointed was a real lack of faith on my part. But now, after what you've said, I wonder… I realize the reality of my feelings. I want a husband, I want children… and those are good things, things that my parents and elders want for me, too. So not getting them *is* a failure, or at least not a *success* .

Maydyn: Wow, yes. I can't imagine. Whenever I imagine someone courting *me,* I always imagine marrying them.

Beth: *[Looks at her phone]* Oh, I need to go now. I hope I've helped.

Maydyn: *[Watching her go]* That must be so hard. I hope *I* don't end up like that.

Isha: I pray you don't.

[The ladies sit without speaking…]

VIII: What are you teaching?

A young man, in his mid to late twenties, enters the park, looking around at the various tables. He sees Sakal sitting alone and, plucking up his courage, walks over to him...

Charles: Excuse me, but are you Mr. Davidson?

Sakal: Why, yes.

Charles: Good. *[Sits down]* Do you have a few minutes? I would like to talk to you.

Sakal: And you are?

Charles: Oh, I'm sorry, I'm Charles, Charles Williamson, the youth pastor at the Terrefille's church.

Sakal: Oh, I see. And you wanted to talk to me?

Charles: Yes, if you don't mind.

Sakal: No, no; I love talking to people. What did you want to talk about?

Charles: Courtship and dating. Not dating, so much, really, courtship.

Sakal: Very well, I am always ready to talk about that. Did you have any questions?

Charles: Oh, no! No, I wanted to set you straight on several things, actually. I heard about your conversations with Andrew, Maydyn and Beth, and was rather disappointed with how poorly it seems they explained courtship to you and your wife.

Sakal: Oh? I thought they did a rather good job, between them. It was rather awkward for them, obviously.

Charles: Yes, you're right. It is awkward for them. They aren't really trained in those things.

Sakal: Those things?

Charles: Well, theology, and youth ministry.

Sakal: I see. I had thought maybe you meant in Bible study and doctrine.

Charles: Yes, that's what I meant by 'theology'.

Sakal: Oh. But you have been trained in those things?

Charles: Yes, I went to seminary. I am their youth pastor.

Sakal: Yes, you told me. So, *revenez a nos moutons,*[lvi] as the French say… where did you feel they failed to explain courtship adequately?

Charles: Ah, yes, well. Let us start from the beginning.

Sakal: A good place.

Charles: Courtship is God's design for bringing together the right young man and the right young woman in marriage at the proper time.

Sakal: Is it?

Charles: Yes! *Courtship brings together Godly principles for the purpose of assuring that a young man and woman should get married to each other. These principles allow them to avoid the pitfalls of dating.*[lvii] Dating is, as you may know, a very dangerous institution that is basically a form of practice for divorce. One pastor said that in dating: *"a young woman gives "a piece of her heart" to a young man when she becomes emotionally involved with him. By the time she meets the man she will marry, she will have only a fragment of her heart left to give. Even without going out on a date, a young woman can give "pieces of her heart" to several young men during her youth, so that by the time she marries, she is no longer [someone who qualifies as] "having been the wife of one man" (1 Tim. 5: 90).*[lviii]

Sakal: That certainly seems to be the implication. But there is really no difference between dating and courting here. Dating and courting *both* encourage these relationships.

Charles: Oh, no, not courting! Courting protects you from those things! Another difference, again to quote a pastor, is that dating encourages people to get involved too young. As he puts it: *"Most young people in the dating culture are nowhere near ready to get married. Mentally, they haven't completed an adequate education. Spiritually, they haven't developed deep convictions necessary for a successful marriage. Financially, they haven't become sufficiently stable to support a new household. Physically and emotionally, they haven't matured in self-discipline to remain one hundred percent pure."*[lix]

Sakal: But they aren't *supposed* to be any of those things before they get married!

Charles: What? They aren't supposed to be pure?

Sakal: No... they aren't supposed to have 'matured in self-discipline to remain one-hundred percent pure.' First of all, no one ever does that, so, taken literally, it would mean that no one should be married. Second of all, it isn't the 'mature' who are supposed to marry, but the immature, the youth.
Experts on courtship write a good deal, but half of what they say isn't even logical, and almost none of it is Biblical.

Charles: You are quite mistaken. Why, much of the conservative church has taken up courtship, or is at least considering it.

Sakal: They are 'courting' courting, eh?

Charles: What? Oh, I see. Yes, quite funny. So you see it *must* be Biblical and logical!

Sakal: No, I don't see that. Why would you even think so? We have had, in the Church and Israel before it, reformation after reformation, turning from things that large sections of the church were teaching, as we discovered their lack of Scriptural support. Why, most of the Church still teaches dating, and you say it is wrong.

Charles: Of course, it's not Biblical.

Sakal: Well, neither is courtship.

Charles: What? But courtship is the Biblical alternative to dating!

Sakal: Well, I would say that courtship is an *un*Biblical alternative to dating.

Charles: That cannot be!

Sakal: It should not be, but it is.

Charles: I don't understand.

Sakal: Let me see if I can explain it in terms you are used to. The same author you quoted earlier, said there are five fundamental principles to what he calls 'Scriptural romance': piety, patriarchy, purity, preparedness and patience.[ix]

Charles: Yes, exactly!

Sakal: And he implies that courtship serves those five ends, and that those ends are the ones we should be seeking in the path to marriage.

Charles: Yes!

Sakal: Except it *doesn't*, and they *aren't*.

Charles: What?!

Sakal: Let's look at them one by one. First of all: 'piety'. Courtship is a modern method of getting married, with no Scriptural examples. From Adam to Christ, no one in Scripture married by courtship. So, at the very least, courtship cannot be the *sole* Godly method of getting married.

Charles: But...

Sakal: Secondly: patriarchy. Courtship is a child driven activity, in which the parents are called on to give their approval or consent. Scripture, on the other hand, speaks of the father of the son 'taking a wife' for his son, and the father of the bride 'giving' her to her husband.[lxi] It gives example after example of young women being given to young men, without the young woman even being consulted; and often, in some of the most Godly marriages in all of Scripture: the marriages of Adam and Isaac, for example, the young man is not consulted.

Charles: Surely you aren't suggesting...

Sakal: Next: purity. It is odd you propose, as a Scriptural method for achieving purity, a system that stands in direct opposition to God's commands through the apostle Paul. In I Corinthians 7, Paul says it is those who do not have sexual self-control who *must* marry. Yet courtship teaches that young people, who want to be married, are supposed to achieve purity and chastity *before* they are allowed to marry. If I have understood them correctly, they would like to re-write I Corinthians 7: 9 to say, 'Better to burn than to marry'.

Charles: It almost sounds as if you were encouraging fornication; that those people who commit fornication are to be rewarded with marriage!

Sakal: No. Paul lays out a dichotomy. First of all, there are people who have the gift of celibacy. They are free to marry, but they are not commanded to. Then, there are those without that gift, the average person, like you and me. These people are given marriage as a gift, a free gift of God. They are given this gift so they can accomplish all of the purposes of marriage, including helping to keep them from fornication.

Charles: But surely before they are married they should remain pure.

Sakal: Surely they should. And just as surely, the primary method God gives for that is for them to get married.
This subject is very frustrating to me. It seems that every time I hear someone preaching about purity and chastity they are not saying, "we are getting them married as fast as we can, but in the meantime..." instead they are saying, "Since they can't get married for a long time after they are physically desirous of it, here are some things we need to do in the, (very long,) meantime."

Charles: Well, those are good things, no? We want them to be focusing on those things!

Sakal: In one sense, yes, in another, no.
If I was talking to a young person, once I convinced them they should be confronting their parents over the issue of Betrothal, then I would definitely be preaching purity and chastity; modest dress and making a covenant with one's eyes.
But the overall discussion on purity and chastity seems to be an exercise in disobedience and frustration.
Let me quote Calvin:
"Since we are reminded by an express declaration, that it is not in every man's power to live chaste in celibacy although it may be his most strenuous study and aim to do so... The Lord prohibits fornication; therefore he requires purity and chastity. The only method which each has of preserving it is to measure himself by his capacity. Let no man rashly despise matrimony as a thing useless or superfluous to him; let no man long for celibacy unless he is able to dispense with the married state... since there are many on whom this blessing is conferred only for a time, let every one, in abstaining from marriage, do it so long as he is fit to endure celibacy. If he has not the power of subduing his passion, let him understand that the Lord has made it obligatory on him to marry.

Charles: What?

Sakal: Basically, if we try to contain our lust by some super spiritual way, if we put off marriage and try to 'do it on our own', he says we war with God[lxii], and God will not help us in our battle.

Charles: That's... I've never heard anyone say that!

Sakal: And yet the church has always taught it. Calvin is by no means alone in this position; Gill, Henry, all the old commentators agree.
Let us turn to the next point: preparedness. The Scriptural injunction is to 'train up the child'[lxiii] and then it is to 'let them marry'.[lxiv] This marriage is said to be in youth,[lxv] and to meet the goals of avoiding fornication,[lxvi] rejoicing in the marriage physically,[lxvii] being fruitful and multiplying,[lxviii] preparing the young man to be an elder,[lxix] and that the wife may do him good and not evil all the days of his life:[lxx] that he may have no need of spoil.[lxxi]
So a 'prepared' young man is one who is young, eager for the pleasures of a wife, just beginning his life as a man, committed to and willing to have children, and needing someone to rejoice with and be good to him.
A 'prepared' young woman is one who is young, just beginning her life as a woman, committed to having children, ready to have her husband rejoice physically with her, and one who is ready to do good to her husband all the days of their lives together.

Charles: I can't believe you are saying these things! They go against *everything* courtship teaches!

Sakal: Quite. Now, on to 'patience'. Patience is a wonderful virtue, but it should not be confused with disobedience or delay. How patient was Abraham's servant?

Charles: Very patient! He went on that long trip...

Sakal: Yes, very patient. But what happened when they tried to feed him?

Charles: He said he needed to tell his business first, and get an answer, before he would eat.[lxxii]

Sakal: And how patient was he the next morning, once Rebecca had been given to Isaac?

Charles: Well, I wouldn't put it quite that way, but he did sort of insist on leaving right away... and did leave right away in spite of everyone arguing with him.[lxxiii]

Sakal: Everyone except Rebecca, and her father.
So I can't say that these five principles actually reflect what Scripture teaches about the path to marriage: at least as they are being applied. I might even propose five different fundamental principles: Godliness, true patriarchy, covenant, youth, and obedience.

Charles: Those, those sound OK, but before we go there, I would like to clear something up. Commentators are quite clear on the fact that Rebecca wasn't just 'given' to Isaac, but she had the final approval over the marriage. You will remember verse 58, of Gen 24 that is, where she says...

Sakal: *"I will go."* Yes, I remember. And do *you* remember verses fifty and fifty one?

Charles: No, that is... just a minute, let me look them up. *And Laban and Bethuel answered and said, The thing has come from Jehovah; we are not able to speak to you good or evil. Behold! Rebekah is before you, take her and go. And let her become the wife of the son of your master, as Jehovah has spoken.*
Yes, of course. But we have to take those verses in the context of verse fifty eight, where they asked Rebecca if she would marry Isaac. As Calvin, I hear you are fond of quoting him, says: *When, however, he had previously offered his daughter, without making any exception, he is to be understood as having done it, only so far as he was able. But now, Moses declares that he did not exercise tyranny over his daughter, so as to thrust her out reluctantly, or to compel her to marry against her will, but left her to her own free choice.*[lxxiv]

Sakal: Yes, Calvin says that. You will be surprised by some other things Calvin says. But you will notice in his commentary that, speaking of context, he completely leaves out the context of the verse.

Let me ask you. If you stood up in front of the entire church and said you would be teaching a class on courtship, at church, every Tuesday evening at eight o'clock, how impressed would the people in your church be if you sent out an email, the next day, saying your wife had decided she didn't want you to teach the course, so it was canceled?

Charles: I would never do that! If I wasn't sure it would be OK, I wouldn't have made the announcement before checking with her.

Sakal: Exactly, so what does that do to Calvin's argument here? Read Bethuel's statement again, and see how much he qualifies it. Does he say, 'If Rebecca agrees'? Does he even imply it?

Charles: Well, no, not really. It is a very strong statement. But no doubt they made strong statements in those days.

Sakal: And no doubt they *meant* them too. Come, you studied those cultures in seminary. How likely is it that an oriental man of his type would have really meant,"…if my daughter agrees" when taking a vow?

Charles: Well. Not very likely. Then why did they ask her?

Sakal: Gill, who still wants to find some 'consent' from Rebecca, says of verse fifty eight: *"the question was not about her marriage of Isaac, that was agreed upon, and she had doubtless given her consent, and which she tacitly did by accepting of the presents, but about taking the journey immediately:*[lxxv]*"* She had already been given to Isaac; they were having an argument about *when* exactly she should leave. Her mother wanted her to stay for a few days of 'goodbyes', and Abraham's servant, the impatient one, wanted them to leave immediately.

Charles: But *everyone* finds some sort of consent in the passage!

Sakal: Yes. Some of them even find it for Isaac.

Charles: Well, that is harder, I'll admit. Scripture definitely doesn't show Isaac giving his consent at any stage of the process. Some commentators say he was asked, but Scripture just doesn't show it.

Sakal: …which brings us to the question of the sufficiency of Scripture.[lxxvi] In order to arrive at their conclusions, courtship advocates have had to add dozens of conjectures and assumptions to Scripture, and ignore much of what Scripture actually does say… particularly in the area of so-called 'purity' and 'consent'.

Charles: Wow. I have never met anyone who argued quite like you do. A lot of it sounds very familiar, but I've never heard anyone willing to take it so far, and treat the Scriptural examples as being really relevant for our own situation. If you would, could you go back to *your* five principles? I would like to hear how you define them.

Sakal: Certainly. Keep in mind that I invented them only as a partial antidote to those other five. My principles were: Godliness, true patriarchy, covenant, youth, and obedience.

Charles: And by Godliness you mean?

Sakal: God-like-ness... acting in the ways God has exampled and taught. God directly arranged two marriages in Scripture: that of Adam and that of Christ. Neither one was or is anything like a courtship in any of the ways we have discussed. Except, I will grant you, that Christ has no physical *need* for his marriage to the church.

Charles: And you don't see courtship as reflecting those examples, or *any* of the other Scriptural examples?

Sakal: No. There are no examples at all of courtship in Scripture. Even the worst of marriages don't apply those principles, and the best ones *certainly* don't...not courtship principles.

Charles: This is hard for me to accept, and I must admit, I don't know of any counter examples. What of your second point. Why call it 'true patriarchy'?

Sakal: In opposition to the false patriarchy of courtship. Scripture does not show the father merely 'giving his permission' for a courtship, or giving his assent to an 'engagement'. Patriarchy means, 'father-rule' and 'ruling' is what Scripture shows the father doing; giving his word, not merely his permission.
We never see the father saying to the young man, 'come convince my daughter to marry you', instead he says, 'you may marry my daughter, she is yours, she belongs to you now'. Courtship speaks of the parents 'involvement'; but can you really say Abraham or Bethuel were merely 'involved' in Isaac and Rebecca's marriage?
And the *young man's* father... well, perhaps we can get into that later, but there are several Biblical principles about the young man's father which courtship completely ignores or violates. What do most courtship advocates even see as the role of the young man's father, except to be one of the people who must 'feel' the marriage is 'right'?

Charles: Well, it is true, the young woman's father is shown as much more important in most courtship models. But, 'coming back to our sheep', as you said earlier, what of the third point? Courtship is *very* big on 'covenant'!

Sakal: Not enough to make it one of their points. But what I mean by covenant is that there should be no relationship between the two people, no 'romantic' relationship, until they are bound in the permanent covenant of betrothal. I read an article in which a young woman who was being courted said, "I tried to be very careful not to fall in love with him until we had gotten engaged."[lxxvii]

Charles: That was good, no?

Sakal: No. She should not have *had* to 'try very hard' to do something absolutely impossible.
The whole problem was that her father encouraged her to enter an impossible relationship... a relationship where two people are 'exploring' the possibility of marriage, where they are even supposed to be starting to become one, yet they are not supposed to give any of themselves to the other in a romantic way!?
Do you remember your quote from before, where you said, *"in dating a young woman gives "a piece of her heart" to a young man when she becomes emotionally involved with him"?* Well, I would say that, in courting, *"a young woman gives 'a piece of her heart' to a young man when she becomes emotionally involved with him."*
How can she avoid it? How can she possibly look at a young man and say, "I wonder if I might want to marry him", without having part of her heart, at least, sigh and say 'yes' and begin forming an attachment? Begin learning his likes, and dislikes, getting to know his friends, his tastes; and letting him slip, little by little into her heart.
As for the young man, well, I don't want to be crude, but what insanity is it to tell a young man, "I want you to consider whether this young woman would make a good wife, but I don't, ever, want you to think about her... being a wife, in the physical sense. I want you only to consider her sterling spiritual qualities and never her marvelous physical form"?

Charles: Well, that would be hard, I grant you, but it is better than dating! Where they...

Sakal: I am not arguing for dating. Scripture rejects dating even more soundly than it rejects courtship. We were speaking of covenant, and I'm saying that a young man should consider a young woman as a future wife only when she is a present wife... when the two are bound in covenant.
Consider the Scriptural examples. There are, as I count them, exactly six Scriptural examples of young men and women having some kind of 'romantic' relationship before they were married... whether it was one or both of them.

Charles: I don't think I like where this is going...

Sakal: You have a seminary degree. Can you tell me the six examples?

Charles: Well, ummm, depending on how you define 'relationship'… *[Sakal waits patiently]* Well, there was Jacob and Rachel… they ended up getting married!

Sakal: And how do you suppose Leah felt about their pre-marital 'relationship'?

Charles: Well, yes, that didn't exactly help Jacob and Leah get off on the right foot.[lxxviii]

Sakal: I should say not! So, who do you have next?

Charles: Well, I hate to call this a relationship, but Shekem fell in love, or lust at least, for Dinah, Jacob's daughter.[lxxix]

Sakal: And what happened?

Charles: He raped her, and he was killed; as was his father and his entire city. And, to the best of our knowledge, *she* never married after that.

Sakal: OK. Next?

Charles: Well David had two relationships like that: one where a girl fell in love with him and one where he fell in lust with a girl.

Sakal: …and they turned out?

Charles: Well, he ended up marrying them later, both of them, but it wasn't the best of situations.[lxxx] In one case her father said she would be a 'snare' to David,[lxxxi] and in the other, David committed adultery with her and then murdered her husband because of his relationship with her.[lxxxii]

Sakal: An excellent summary, and two more bad examples to learn from. Next?

Charles: There's Amnon, who 'loved' his sister Tamar and raped her. He ended up getting killed by her brother.[lxxxiii] And then Samson, who God caused to lust after a Philistine girl in order to slay the Philistines. As well as the girl, and her father, and his best man…[lxxxiv]

Sakal: So, all of the examples we have from Scripture of pre-marital relationships are negative. They demonstrate the importance of being bound in covenant *before* thinking of someone as your wife or husband, or having any kind of romantic involvement.

Charles: Wow, that's a harsh conclusion! I disagree, of course. I can't throw out the idea of the couple having some kind of relationship before they are married: it goes against everything I have been taught; everything that *anyone* is teaching. But I can see where you get it from Scripture! Covenant is a very important concept, and the examples of pre-marital relationships are all very problematic.
But what about 'youth'? Although I don't really need to ask that, do I?

Scripture certainly speaks of marriage in the youth, and most of what marriage is supposed to accomplish is best started in youth. I remember, my wife and I, we took a couple years to work out exactly how we wanted to live together as a couple and most of which was getting rid of habits we'd picked up while unmarried. So what about 'obedience'? Courtship is all about being obedient!

Sakal: No, courtship is all about being 'patient'. It replaces difficult obedience with frustrated patience.

We are teaching our girls to desire to be wives and mothers, and our boys to be husbands and fathers, yet, once they get old enough for their bodies to begin telling them that it is time for them to do exactly that, we tell them to 'wait'. We totally abdicate our role as father's in actually 'taking wives for our sons' or 'giving our daughters in marriage'.

But it goes beyond that. Courtship does not just say 'wait', but deliberately says 'not yet', 'not now', 'not you', or 'not them'. Think of how much of each sermon or book on courtship is about reasons why they shouldn't get engaged, shouldn't court, aren't ready yet, how that person isn't the 'right person'; or how everyone needs to wait on the proper 'feelings'.

Charles: Well, yes, of course.

Sakal: 'Of course' what? What is Scriptural about it? How does that promote marriage in youth? Or the principle of 'letting them marry'?

Charles: But we can't just, they can't just... marry!

Sakal: Why ever not? Is it not written, *"it is not good for man to be alone"*?[lxxxv] Should we patiently wait in disobedience to a clear Biblical Principle? Does Jesus or Paul indicate it has been repealed in the New Testament?

Charles: No, far from it.

Sakal: Well then, that is what I mean by 'obedience'. We are clearly commanded *not* to 'wait' on marriages, but to act *toward* them: to take wives for our sons, give our daughters in marriage; and 'let them marry'.[lxxxvi] Instead we 'wait on the Lord' in clear disobedience to His commands!

Charles: Wow. This is a lot for me to take in all at once. Can we meet again, tomorrow?

Sakal: Sure. *[The two shake hands gravely, and the youth pastor pulls out his cell phone as he walks away.]*

IX: To avoid fornication.

Sakal: *[Comes over to where Charles is sitting]* We meet again?

Charles: Oh, Mr. Davidson! Yes. Please, have a seat. Thank you for coming.
If you don't mind, I'd like to really focus, today, on something that you implied yesterday. Much of your argument for young marriages seemed to focus on the issue of, well, fornication. Mental fornication, I assume you mean?

Sakal: Mental or physical.

Charles: Wow! So you mean…? Well, let's not go there, not today.[lxxxvii]
I read up on the I Corinthians 7: 2 passage, which seems most critical to what you are saying. I read a number of sermons on the subject, and most of the authors that I read were in agreement that verse two, which at first blush seems to say that every man should have his own wife,[lxxxviii] actually means that married men should have their own wives. That it is actually a summary of verses three through five which speak of a man and his wife, in the physical sense.

Sakal: So you're saying that verse two means, 'In order to avoid fornication, let each man who is already married sleep with his own wife'?

Charles: Well, yes, when put crudely.

Sakal: And verse nine?

Charles: Verse nine? I was talking about verse two.

Sakal: And your explanation for verse two (which, as you say, flies in the face of its clear meaning) founders on the rocks of verse nine. Surely you can't mean 'let every man who is already married marry and not burn'?

Charles: But I *can* mean that, and you have shown me how. I am becoming more and more convinced by this thing you call 'betrothal', instead of 'engagement'. And many courtship advocates talk of it as well. Verse nine could be speaking of a betrothed couple, who are getting a little too eager to come together, or maybe they have already done so, surreptitiously; saying that they need to marry.

Sakal: And verse thirty six?

Charles: Well verse thirty six does definitely help with your 'young marriage' argument. But really, we all want that. But our children need to be prepared before they marry. So verse thirty six, which talks about a girl who is passing 'the flower of her age', is definitely in favor of young marriages... but not unprepared ones, and it says nothing about the temptation or 'burning' issues of the previous verses.

Sakal: Well, I would argue with that, but it seems to me there is a basic logic flaw in your argument as well.

Charles: Well, it's not really my argument, many of the sermons that I read...

Sakal: ...and none of the old commentaries. In a minute I will tell you what Calvin said on this issue... and John Gill, and Matthew Henry. But let us look at the logic flaw first.

Verse two speaks of 'avoiding fornication', verse nine speaks of a lack of 'self-control' or, as the KJV puts it, an inability to 'contain'. Certainly the married man, and the betrothed man, may have issues with both of these problems, issues which may be helped by coming together on a regular basis with his wife.

But is it only, or even principally, the married and betrothed men who have problems with fornication and lust? Does it make sense, really, to say 'in order for the married man to have relief from the temptation of fornication he should sleep with his wife, but the unmarried man can be perfectly content without one? Do you know many, or any, young men who are not troubled by lust? Do you know of anywhere else in Scripture where, except for the gift that Christ and Paul[lxxxix] talk about, a young man is able to get relief from this?

Charles: But no one believes that this means that the unmarried man *must* marry!

Sakal: Until recently, practically *everyone* believed it. Calvin is particularly forceful on the subject. He says: *... The incontinent, therefore, neglecting to cure their infirmity by this means, sin by the very circumstance of disobeying the Apostle's command. ....*[xc]

Charles: Oh. But...

Sakal: And lest you think he was alone in this, John Gill says: *if either therefore they want a will or power to contain, let them marry; it is not only lawful for them to marry, but it is right and best for them;* [xci] Matthew Henry says: *not law bound a man to marry so that he sinned if he did not; I mean, unless his circumstances required it for preventing the lust of uncleanness.* And he says: *This is God's remedy for lust. The fire may be quenched by the means he has appointed.*[xcii] And then: *marriage, with all its inconveniences, is much better than to burn with impure and lustful desires. Marriage is honourable in all; but it is a duty in those who cannot contain nor conquer those inclinations.*[xciii]

Charles: But how, why... why is no one saying that nowadays?

Sakal: Well, some Godly men are.[xciv] But the reason that I see is because we are Gnostic.

Charles: Gnostic?! We believe in a spirit/mind duality, with the body being basically bad?

Sakal: Yes. And do you see how it applies to this issue?

Charles: I, umm, I'm almost afraid to say that I do.

Sakal: What do you see?

Charles: That these earlier commentators, they really believed that marriage was, that… *[Sakal waits patiently]*
This is so hard to say. Nowadays we see the spiritual problem of fornication, lust and adultery, and we seek a spiritual solution… more Bible study, more prayer, an increase in faith, repentance, etc. But these old commentators seem to be insisting that I Corinthians 7:2-5 says that a man should seek a solution to their spiritual problem with a physical solution. That we should seek relief…
Oh, Hi Andrew! *[Blushing furiously]*

Andrew: Pastor Charles! And sitting here talking with Mr. Davidson! What is the occasion?

Sakal: *[Seeing that Charles is embarrassed]* We were having another discussion about courtship. We were discussing…

Charles: *[Clears his throat loudly]* Actually, I would like to discuss what you said the other day about engagement.

Sakal: Very well, although it is not that difficult a subject. I dislike the word 'engagement' because it fails to reflect the reality of the relationship.

Andrew: Yeah. I looked that one up, too. A lot of commentators talk about it, although most of them feel comfortable using both words. But they talk about the differences, how engagement is a 'lighter' term, that pretty much everyone sees your being able to get out of, whereas betrothal, or espousal, is permanent, like marriage vows.

Sakal: Exactly. *[He and Andrew both look at Charles]* Does that answer your question?

Charles: *[Huskily]* Yes.

Sakal: Well, good. So getting back to our previous subject, Proverbs five speaks of the exact same thing. It says that a young man who is enjoying his own wife is, or should be, 'distracted' from other women.[xcv] And the church is afraid of that idea. They want our young men to be pure, to have conquered lust, before they even think about marriage.

Andrew: Don't I know it!

Charles: But don't you want our young men, and women, to be pure?

Sakal: Of course I do. And the way that Scripture says that that should happen is that they should marry; and courtship seems to contradict that or, at the very least, to delay it.

Charles: But so much of my training has been designed to help find ways to help young men deal with the problem of lust. It is one of the biggest issues in Youth Pastoring!

Sakal: Oh?

Andrew: *[Giggles]*

Charles: *[Looking from one to the other]* But you seem to be saying we *shouldn't* be working on combating lust.

Andrew: *[Sakal looks at Andrew, who grins]* No, pastor, he isn't saying that at all. He is saying you *should* be working on combating lust... by helping us get married when we need it, and not years later.

Charles: But I'm a youth pastor, not a matchmaker!

Sakal: Maybe you need to change jobs.[xcvi] God's Word teaches that our young people are to get married in order to 'combat lust'. It isn't the only thing they need to do; our society, including our churches, needs to change in very significant ways.
But if we ignore or deny the method that God insists upon the most strongly, indeed the only method that he specifically relates for this issue, then how can we ask for his help? That was Calvin's point: that if we seek to conquer our sins, but ignore what God has said about how to do so, we 'war with God' and 'resist his ordinances'. He calls it 'vain' and 'presumptuous'.

Charles: But what does that have to do with me? It isn't like I have a son or daughter that age.

Sakal: I believe that each of us should have our role in obeying the command of I Corinthians 7:2. For example:
Young children: These should be, under their parents guidance, getting ready to be married themselves, keeping themselves pure and focused on brother/sister relationships, encouraging and rejoicing with their older siblings as they marry and have children. Older children: Should hold themselves in readiness; eagerly anticipating marriage while insisting on holding each brother and sister in the church as exactly that in all purity; waiting with eager obedience for the day when their father will present them with a spouse.
Childless (or pregnant) Couples: Praying for and otherwise uplifting and encouraging and assisting the others in the church as they are able in this area.

Older Couples: They should do the same things as the childless couples, and the older women should be teaching the young women as we learn about in Titus 2.

The Elders: Teaching the Word of God on this issue; particularly in light of the current false teachings of courtship and dating; rebuking and admonishing their congregations when necessary; helping their church to be salt and light on this issue wherever possible; specifically facilitating marriages, young marriages, fruitful young marriages. Counseling and encouraging the resulting marriages.

Fathers of Sons: Teaching their sons to be prepared for the wife they will bring them; determining their need for marriage; actively seeking a wife for their sons; taking wives for their sons from daughters who have need, where necessary.

Fathers of Daughters: Teaching their daughters to be ready for the husband they will bring them; determining their need for marriage; giving their daughters in marriage: either to a son who has need or, if their daughter herself has a need, even to a son who has not need.

Charles: Wow, that is a heavy list, and a heavy burden. Can we talk again later?

Sakal: Certainly. *[Charles wanders off and Andrew and Sakal sit for a few minutes more...]*

X: A Deliberate Question.

We find Charles and Sakal sitting together.

Charles: I found that last conversation very awkward once Andrew had arrived. I don't think we should be talking about such things around unmarried young men... or women of course!

Sakal: Well, I don't have any such quibbles,[xcvii] and I think they should be married.

Charles: But, listen, I think you weren't really fair to the courtship advocates.

Sakal: Oh?

Charles: You seemed to be implying that they were deliberately exposing their children to the temptation of fornication and lust.

Sakal: I see those as the same temptation, but putting that aside, you use a word, 'deliberate' which can mean at least two different things. Firstly, it can mean 'slowly'; and secondly it can mean 'intentionally'. You must at least admit that the method is slow.

Charles: Well, yes. I hadn't really thought so before but now that we've talked about it, well, there do seem to be a lot of older 'young people' in our churches.
But surely you aren't saying it is intentional?

Sakal: Well, yes and no... and yes. I doubt there is anyone out there (except Satan) who is saying to themselves, "I like this courtship system because it promotes lust." But the system itself *does* promote lust, and in a way that is directly contrary to what Scripture tells us to do. So it is a deliberate system, and it does promote lust.
Indeed, some courtship advocates even hint at this. Douglas Wilson is brave enough to point out that courtship is a sexual relationship. Indeed, he even calls it a 'volatile sexual relationship'.[xcviii] He then says, that the term courtship, it's etymology, has it's origin in practices just as unbiblical as dating. Courtship, as it was originally practiced, was where a variety of vain young men convinced other men's wives to commit adultery with them.[xcix]

Charles: That certainly isn't the way we teach it nowadays!

Sakal: True, and I'm not accusing you of that. But it is important to recognize that that is where the term courtship originates: that it comes from a system of organized adultery; hardly an auspicious beginning.

The system was designed, from its beginning, to encourage lust, and no amount of changes can take away that essential character from it.

Charles: That's a very harsh accusation. Just because a word began by describing a process that was unGodly doesn't mean that we can't use that term to describe a Godly thing.

Sakal: Oh? Can you? If you use a word that has unGodly connotations, will not everyone who hears it hear the unGodly meaning? Is there really any way to put a hedge around a word and prevent it's previous meanings from coming through?

Charles: Well, perhaps you're right. But, what was your second, 'yes'?

Sakal: That is the hardest of all. The courtship system does, really, look at a young man who admits to lust, or fornication, and they really, seriously, and deliberately tell him 'too bad, you can't have a wife'. It is actually down in black and white, in book after book, on website after website… if you don't have victory over lust or fornication, you cannot get married.

Charles: You brought that up the other day. But surely… How can you…?

Sakal: *[Waits patiently for a minute, then says]* How can I give my 'innocent' daughter to such a man?

Charles: Yes!

Sakal: First of all, I doubt she is all that innocent. She may be naïve, that certainly seems to be the case amongst the young people in your churches… the ones that haven't fallen to fornication already, that is. But she isn't sinless any more than he is. Perhaps she is even a worse sinner, it is God who judges the heart, not us.[c] And, again, it doesn't matter. Scripture is absolutely clear on this… that is the kind of man that needs a wife.[ci] The modern church's view seems to be that we should only give water to someone who has conquered thirst, or preach the gospel to someone who has conquered sin.[cii]

Charles: But surely you aren't saying that we should reward their sin with a wife!

Sakal: I am saying almost the opposite! Do you think that was what John Calvin was saying? Surely not!

Charles: Well, what can that mean then?

Sakal: It means that the young man… or woman, but most of us focus on the young man, who finds himself tempted, or even finds himself sinning, in a sexual area, is obligated to not only repent in the usual way… admit his sin, be sorry for it, etc. but he is also obligated to turn to the remedy that God Himself has designed for that sin. His very seeking of a wife is an act of repentance.

Charles: Wow. I'd never looked at it in that way. But, coming back... you are not saying that courtship is deliberately trying to promote lust as in 'intentionally' trying to promote lust, but rather that it *is* promoting lust, and doing so with deliberate policies, policies that are unScriptural, and that Scripture says *will* promote lust.

Sakal: Yes. And those same policies are denying young people husbands and wives and thus denying them the other benefits of marriage. Young men do not have helpmeets; young women are not bearing children. They are all being denied the companion of their youth. You mentioned earlier that there are many young men and women not married in your church. Be honest: how many, and how old?

Charles: Well, several, and some are over twenty-five, a couple are getting up to thirty.

Sakal: And that doesn't make you sad? Are these young people that aren't married, are they the dregs of the church; the ones into pornography or fornication?

Charles: No! Some of them are the best in our church; the sons and daughters of the elders and deacons!

Sakal: And that doesn't tell you something?

Charles: What could it... oh. You mean that many of those who are following courtship the most strictly aren't getting married?

Sakal: Exactly.

Charles: But how can that be? How can so many Godly men be getting it so wrong?

Sakal: Well, you are a Presbyterian, surely you know the motto 'Semper Reformada'? Our society, years ago, began moving away from Scriptural principles in marriage, and we need to 'keep reforming' and move back.

Charles: Wow. I know just what you mean. I was watching this film the other day and it was full of wonderful quotes, all of which said the same thing, basically: we need to go back to what Scripture teaches. One man said, *"And it occurred to me, that the structure of ministry that I was promoting was contrary to Scripture, and that it was harming the next generation and dividing the church. And I realized that those things that we were trusting in had failed us. The crux of the matter is that progressively, over the last two hundred years, the church has set aside the sufficiency of Scripture for the discipleship of the next generation."*[ciii] He was talking about something entirely different, but I can see how it applies here. The same man said, *"God's patterns are transcultural, they work in every culture, because they're from God. Our people, all people have the same sin natur, but God's Word is true in every culture."*[civ]

It scared me, that film. And especially one particular quote, where one pastor said that he had been teaching on a very difficult subject, a very controversial subject and… *"A man stood up in the congregation. He said "[Pastor], if I do these things, that I know are right, my church will kill me!" And I looked at him, and I said "Then die.""*[cv]

Sakal: God calls us to do hard things… but then he makes those hard things light.[cvi] We need to look at what God's Word says, and follow that, no matter what the world says or does… or the rest of the church, for that matter. We are to be salt and light in this matter as much as any other…

Charles: But…surely you can't be saying that we should have no qualifications at all? What of examples of Caleb and Saul? They had qualifications.

Sakal: *[Laughing]* I'm not sure how the courtship crowd would appreciate your analogy. "Come marry my daughter if you take this city," or "Come take my daughter if you kill one hundred Philistines." Those aren't exactly the kind of vague and spiritual qualifications that they tend to look for.

Charles: And… and there is another difference. I never really thought of this before.

Sakal: Oh?

Charles: Yes. They were positive, not negative qualifications. They were how you *could* marry their daughter… "If you accomplish this you *can* marry my daughter." They weren't negative qualifications, they weren't preventing marriage, they were encouraging it.
Caleb didn't say, "Unless you take this city you can't marry my daughter," he said, "*If* you take the city you *can*." There are probably a lot of young men who, set such a challenge, an open, honest challenge by the father, would actually rise to the challenge, and take the city, or pay the fee, or whatever it is.

Sakal: That is an important difference. The pastor who said that the man who marries his daughter must be 'elder material'… I don't see how any young man could but see that as a roadblock. It isn't like they could just rush out and do something about it!

Charles: But you can't be saying that you don't have any qualifications!?

Sakal: Oh, yes. I have the qualifications that are implied in I Corinthians 7:2.

Charles: But, but it says *every* man!

Sakal: And it says that to the church. So every 'church' man. Every believer, in fellowship with his church. I have no obligations toward non-believers, not in this way; nor to members under discipline, cast out from their church.

And it uses the terms 'husband' and 'wife'. Back in Bible times this might not have been an issue, but before I give my daughter to some young man I want to be assured that he understands what 'marriage' is, his obligations and responsibilities.

Charles: What do you mean? People today understand what 'married' means.

Sakal: Do they? That might make a whole new conversation... what marriage actually is, and whether modern people, modern Christians understand it.

But your question here was about my qualifications. Both of these qualifications are those that are positive: any young man can meet them. Turn to Christ, repent, believe, and show an understanding of marriage. And I make these qualifications public.

But the courtship qualifications are not so. First of all, they are rarely public; and second, they are rarely attainable in any kind of overt, objective way. What young man in your church would be willing to stand up and say, "I claim your daughter as my wife, I have met the qualifications..." the way David did?

Charles: I don't have a daughter! That is, she is two!

Sakal: Not yours, then, the other men in your church. How many have taken the Caleb challenge and 'published' their qualifications; and even if they had, how many of those qualifications are objective and attainable?

Charles: *[After a pause]* None of them. Either way.

Sakal: So, if you were the father of a young man in your church, and you were looking at the various young ladies in the church, to how many of those father's would you feel comfortable going and saying, "My son fits your qualifications, give her to me for him!"?

Charles: I don't have a son... but... even if I were to pick the most Godly son of our church, I doubt I would feel comfortable doing that!

Sakal: So, the example of Caleb doesn't exactly help, does it? Or David?

Charles: But why do you suppose they are doing this?

Sakal: I have no idea, really. Scripture is full of marriage passages; many of which are commands. "Be fruitful and multiply", "It is not good for man to be alone."

Charles: "He who finds a wife finds a good thing, and obtains favor from the Lord." "She shall do him good and not evil all the days of his life."

Sakal: So, we are agreed on that?

Charles: Yes, actually. You have given me a lot to think about; much of which I already knew, but have never put together in this way. Thanks.

Sakal: Anytime...

XI: Courting Parents.

Sakal is sitting at the table reading, when Andrew approaches him.

Andrew: Hey, Mr. Davidson?

Sakal: Hello Andrew, what's up? *[The two shake hands as Andrew sits down.]*

Andrew: Maydyn and I were talking and she was telling me about her conversations with your wife.

Sakal: Yes?

Andrew: I was wondering if that wasn't another difference between courting and dating. We touched on it, but…

Sakal: Yes?

Andrew: The whole parental authority thing. It isn't just that I needed permission to court her, but that it was really her father that I had to convince that I could marry her, and not just her. We talked about it and decided that maybe one difference was that courtship was 'parent driven' and dating was 'couple driven'.

Sakal: That might be a difference, certainly. You don't have the parents going out on the dates, but…

Andrew: They are supposed to be the ones making the decision, at least, along with the couple. Her parents, and even, she said, my parents.

Sakal: So, you two would continue to date until one of your parents decided that you should be married, and then you would get married?

Andrew: Umm, no, sort of the opposite if anything. We would date until we thought we should get married, and then, if everyone else felt it was right, then we would get married.

Sakal: And if they didn't?

Andrew: What?

Sakal: If they didn't all feel it was right.

Andrew: Then we wouldn't get married.

Sakal: You would go on dating?

Andrew: Well, I don't know. She wasn't real clear on that. I kind of got the idea that, if they really didn't feel it was right, we would have to stop courting and just go try someone else.

Sakal: After spending a week or so dating Maydyn?

Andrew: Oh, not a *week*! Courtships are much longer than that.

Sakal: Oh... why?

Andrew: Because you have to decide if you are the right people to marry, and whether God will be glorified in your marriage.

Sakal: And that takes a long time?

Andrew: Of course.

Sakal: Why?

Andrew: What do you mean, why? Because it does. How long did it take you?

Sakal: Oh, but I didn't court Isha... not until after I was betrothed to her, anyway, and I think that is different from what you are thinking about. Indeed, our betrothal day was the first time I had ever seen her.

Andrew: What? That's crazy!

Sakal: Do you think I have a bad wife?

Andrew: What? No, no. I've never met her but Maydyn says she is just wonderful.

Sakal: So why is it crazy? What is there about dating for a week, a month, or six months, that will make you a better husband, or her a better wife?

Andrew: That's not the point.

Sakal: Oh? Then why is what Isha and I did crazy?

Andrew: Well, I guess, if it works for you but...

Sakal: 'Works for you'?! Is *that* the way you apply God's Word to your life? Whatever 'works for you'?

Andrew: *[Blushes]* I didn't mean that, I just meant that... I don't know what I mean. How could you *do* that?

Sakal: Do what? Love my wife? [cvii]

Andrew: No, marry someone you didn't even know. People have to get to know each other first, to be friends.[cviii]

Sakal: So you see 'friendship' as the first part of the path to marriage?

Andrew: Yes, of course. You can't marry someone unless you are friends first!

Sakal: I did.

Andrew: But you came from a different culture. We can't, we Americans.

Sakal: Because it isn't right, or for some other reason?

Andrew: Because it isn't right!
The whole goal of courtship, or dating for that matter, is to get to the point where the couple after an adequate time [together], are quite sure that they love each other deeply; that in every way they were made for each other, and God's seal is upon their union, [and for them] to prepare for marriage![cix]

Sakal: So why is that? Why can't you just choose someone off the street, or roll the dice?

Andrew: Because it must be the *right* person. Look, Maydyn and I found this old sermon on courtship. And it gave four principles that it said must guide our choice. 1) Choose a Christian, 2) Choose a Kindred Spirit, 3) Look for Character, 4) Look for Accomplishments. Don't those sound wonderful?[cx]

Sakal: They certainly do. But your list leaves me wondering two things. First of all, is this list itself Biblical: do the Scriptures say that only people like this may be married? And second, does the Scripture tell you, yourself, to do the choosing?

Andrew: Well, I hope the first one is obvious, anyway. Of course she must be a Christian. Isn't it written, *"In the Lord?"*[cxi]

Sakal: It certainly is. It is also written not to be unequally yoked, although the context is not at all marriage[cxii], and it cannot seriously have been intended to be applied to marriage.[cxiii]

Andrew: Well, good then, so a boy must choose a Christian girl... a Christian boy, that is.

Sakal: If the boy is to choose, it certainly seems that that would be a wise choice.

Andrew: What do you mean, 'if the boy is to choose'?

Sakal: Again, your list presumes that it is the boy himself who will do the choosing. And it also presumes he has a choice.

Andrew: Who else would choose for him? She is to be *his* wife!

Sakal: Well, you know your Scriptures. How often was it that the boy, himself, chose his wife?

Andrew: Well, there was... there was Esau and his, ummm, wives.[cxiv]

Sakal: Yes.

Andrew: Not that he was the best example… and he didn't exactly marry a Christian, or a believer, anyway.

Sakal: No, not as far as we know. Are there any other examples?

Andrew: Well, lot's of guys are said to have 'taken a wife'.

Sakal: Including Isaac.

Andrew: Well, yes, so perhaps that doesn't mean quite what we take it to mean. David, he chose, well, he chose to fight for his wife![cxv]

Sakal: Yes, as did Othniel… after the father of the girl offered her[cxvi]. Good examples, sort of. Now, what of the other side? How many boys in Scripture did not choose their own wives?

Andrew: Well, Adam, of course. Isaac. Jacob with Leah. He didn't exactly pick Zilpah and Bilhah. And then there was… well, OK, there are lots of guys in Scripture who didn't pick their own wives.[cxvii]

Sakal: What of Christ?

Andrew: Yes, that's a very good example. Christ chose us![cxviii]

Sakal: Oh?

Andrew: What do you mean…? Oh, well, that's right. He chose us, because his father told him to choose us[cxix].

Sakal: So, what have we learned?

Andrew: That the boy doesn't always get to pick his own wife. But he has to agree, doesn't he? And so he should refuse a non-Christian! It isn't even a marriage if it is a non-Christian; like in the time of Ezra.[cxx]

Sakal: Oh? Perhaps if we re-read what Peter says to wives?

Andrew: Let me look it up. Oh, wow, I had forgotten that passage:
1 Peter 3:1-6 *Likewise, ye wives, be in subjection to your own husbands; that, if any obey not the word, they also may without the word be won by the conversation of the wives; While they behold your chaste conversation coupled with fear. Whose adorning let it not be that outward adorning of plaiting the hair, and of wearing of gold, or of putting on of apparel; But let it be the hidden man of the heart, in that which is not corruptible, even the ornament of a meek and quiet spirit, which is in the sight of God of great price. For after this manner in the old time the holy women also, who trusted in God, adorned themselves, being in subjection unto their own husbands: Even as Sara obeyed Abraham, calling him lord: whose daughters ye are, as long as ye do well, and are not afraid with any amazement.*
But that is after they are married. Surely no Christian could accept a wife who wasn't a Christian!

Sakal: I suppose that depends on how you view marriage. If your father, or the king, chose a wife for you, do you think that is a covenant? Or is he just expressing his preference, something you are free to go against?

Andrew: Wow. That's a hard question. And I'm afraid I won't like the answer. I keep thinking about Esther.[cxxi] She couldn't have married the pagan, uncircumcised king, it was totally against the law; and she would never have wanted to marry him anyway. But what if she didn't have a choice, unless it wasn't her that 'married' him? What if she was 'married' by the king himself, and that was what made their covenant?

Sakal: Yes. And the Scriptures keep using a very awkward phrase, "take wives for your sons". What of Joseph[cxxii], or Moses[cxxiii]?

Andrew: Those are awkward examples too. Both of those men, Godly men, married daughters of priests, pagan priests… it isn't very likely that those girls were the sole believers in their father's household. And, the way the Scripture puts it, it doesn't look like either of them took the initiative, but that they were married by someone else: Joseph by Pharaoh or Moses by his father-in-law Jethro.

Sakal: And, of course, there is the example of Hosea.[cxxiv]

Andrew: Hosea?! He married a…

Sakal: Prostitute?

Andrew: (Nods)

Sakal: Did *she* meet any of those qualities?

Andrew: No, but that's not a fair test. God Himself told Hosea who to marry.

Sakal: And?

Andrew: Well, that makes it not a fair test. We have to figure out who to marry on our own.

Sakal: Do we? God's Word gives us no clues?

Andrew: Well, every time we seem to get a clue, you seem to find some example that denies it, or some teaching that contradicts it.

Sakal: …which should be a clue that our clue is, perhaps, not right; or not absolute. If someone says, "No Christian may ever do this," and then they list something that many Godly men *did* do, that is a hint that perhaps the 'no Christian' part was wrong. No one is saying that one should go out of your way to marry a non-believer. But God makes it clear that some believers, at some times, did do so… and that God expected them to honor their marriage vow.

Andrew: So why did they marry them at all? *[Pulls out his phone, looks at it]* Oh, wow, I need to go. Can we talk tomorrow?

Sakal: Certainly, I'll be here.

XII: A Help 'meet'.

Andrew: Hey, Mr. Davidson.

Sakal: Hello.

Andrew: Well, last night, before bed... actually I stayed up kind of late...I got out my concordance and looked up what we were talking about and I may have to admit defeat.
It certainly does look like, in Bible times at least, the father could choose a wife for his son, or a king for someone else, and even a believer would marry the girl they were given, even if she wasn't a believer. And the law did the same thing, choosing a wife for someone when a brother died, regardless of their spiritual state, or qualifications, or anything.[cxxv]

Sakal: So, what is your conclusion?

Andrew: It is definitely *best* to marry a believer, but if you don't, or if someone else marries you, like they used to do in the old days, it is still a marriage, and you have to honor it, honor your wife.
Several times in Scripture it seems that someone else chose a wife for a Godly man and the Godly man married them, even though it seems like they weren't believers or even Israelites.
Scripture makes it seem as if the choosing or giving itself creates some sort of bond...

Sakal: An interesting idea. It looks like you have something to chew on there. What was the second point in the list of things the girl has to be?

Andrew: A 'kindred spirit'.

Sakal: That sounds very odd. What do you mean by it?

Andrew: Well, *I* didn't say it but it made sense when I heard it. A guy and a girl have to be right for each other when they go into marriage. Their personalities, their interests, need to mesh.

Sakal: Oh?

Andrew: I am learning to hate it when you do that (grins). So, you would ask me to prove that from Scripture. And, of course, I won't be able to find anywhere where God says anything... wait, what about in Genesis where God says *"I will make a help meet for [Adam]"*?[cxxvi] 'Meet' means 'appropriate for', no?

Sakal: And?

Andrew: And what? So that must mean that Eve was 'meet' for Adam.

Sakal: I agree.

Andrew: So that must mean that when we pick a wife, or get given a wife, we need to pick a kindred spirit!

Sakal: Or it could mean the opposite.

Andrew: What? Oh. You mean… you mean when we pick a wife she *is* a kindred spirit, she *is* meet.

Sakal: *'He who finds a wife…'*

Andrew: *'… finds a good thing, and obtains favor from the Lord.'*[cxxvii] Not, 'he who finds the perfect wife', or 'a kindred wife'. I know. That particular verse has been hammering itself into my brain recently. That and *'it is not good for man to be alone'.*[cxxviii]

Sakal: *[Grins]* Yes. And, as husbands we are to love our wives; a Biblical process which, if followed, will bind their spirits together, making them 'kindred' indeed.
What was the next item on your list?

Andrew: The next two were, 'look for character' and 'look for accomplishments'. But those really are the same thing, the same category as the first two things we talked about. They are great things, but they're not great things that we are required, by Scripture, to seek in a wife. God lists the character and accomplishments of a wife as things the wife, herself, does… not things she does when she is unmarried.[cxxix] And I'm not sure how much in the way of character or accomplishments I *deserve* in a wife. How much in the way of those things do *I* have?

Sakal: There is another issue. I was visiting one of your large stores the other day, and when I walked down the cereal aisle, I saw a hundred choices… just for cereal to eat for breakfast.

Andrew: *[Chuckles]* They don't have that where you come from, eh?

Sakal: No. And I am wondering if *you* have it?

Andrew: What do you mean? I had Apple Jacks just this morning.

Sakal: I wonder if they had character or accomplishments. But I meant in our area, our discussion. Are there hundreds of girls lined up on a shelf somewhere for you to pick from, all of whom would immediately agree to marry you? Or who would even agree to marry you after an extended courtship?

Andrew: *[Blushing]* You really know how to tease a guy. I know some great girls… and some not so great girls… but I'm not such a stud as to have a hundred girls on my list.

Sakal: That was not what I meant. Even if you only have five girls on your 'list', would they all agree to marry you?

Andrew: Well, umm, that is part of what we do in dating, you know. Or courtship, I suppose. We find that out.

Sakal: So even if you were to find the most perfect girl in the country; one who fit a list not of four points but of seventeen points, she still might not want to marry you.

Andrew: If she was *that* perfect, I am *sure* she wouldn't want to! Not *me*, anyway!

Sakal: So then, the list seems to me to be rather a roadblock against marriage.

Andrew: And you are already married! You should see how it looks from here!

Sakal: You are finding it frustrating; the process of looking for a wife?

Andrew: Especially after talking with you. You seem to throw everything I always knew out the window.

Sakal: Well, it is written, *"Faithful are the wounds of a friend; but the kisses of an enemy are deceitful."*[cxxx]
Let us look at it from the opposite direction. Suppose of those five girls, the one's that you know, you find only one who would marry you, and she does not fit your seventeen, or even your four, points?

Andrew: I guess I would have to start again, and meet more girls.

Sakal: And she, having gone through the process with you, would have to go out and meet more boys.

Andrew: Yeah.

Sakal: Further delaying marriage.

Andrew: You're telling me. You're making it sound like I might be *fifty* before I get married!

Sakal: That is, indeed, what it sounds like. Are you happy with that?

Andrew: Of course not!

Sakal: Do you think it is what God intends?

Andrew: I don't see how it can be. He says, *'it is not good for man to be alone'...*[cxxxi]and this makes it sound like 'alone' is exactly what I'll be!

Sakal: That was my impression as well.

Andrew: But what choice do I have? I *want* a 'wife of my youth', but how do I *get* a 'wife of my youth'?

Sakal: Well, let us go back to our question of the other day. You say that courtship is parent driven, and dating is couple driven. So, would you add that to your definition of the other day? Would you now say that courting is: 'A parent-driven process where a boy comes to a girl's father, and says he wants to date her seriously, as part of an entire process, with a view toward a covenant marriage, and promises that there would be no physical involvement until they were married?'

Andrew: Yeah, maybe. I'll have to ask Maydyn or her dad. What do you think?

Sakal: I think that the definition still has the word 'date' in it, and doesn't solve our issues at all.

Andrew: So, that would make courting a subset of 'ways to date'... just like there are people who 'date' by sleeping with everyone in sight. And courtship is a method that seems to specialize in delaying or preventing marriages, not creating them.
Say, would you mind meeting with Maydyn's father? He says that he would really like to talk to you, that he hasn't heard anyone saying quite what you are.

Sakal: Gladly. Would you like to bring him to dinner at our house tonight? And his wife and children, if he wishes.

Andrew: I wouldn't want to put you out...

Sakal: No, my wife loves entertaining. She and my children will be thrilled.

Andrew: That would be great! *[Pulls out his phone, and Sakal grins as he watches Andrew walk away.]*

XIII: An (overly) Eager Young Man.

Kitchen scene with large table, lots of kids, including Andrew, Maydyn, her family, Sakal, and his family.

Pat: That was a great dinner, thanks!

Sakal: No problem. We were glad to have you over.

Pat: It was really nice to invite all of us over.

Sakal: Well, when you have eight children, adding four or five more people to a meal is no big deal.

Pat: You must have a very patient wife to be willing to have that many children.[cxxxii]

Sakal: I do have a very patient wife... after all, she married me.

Pat: *[Laughs]* Say, would you mind going on a walk with me, just the two of us?

Sakal: No, that would be fine. *[The two walk outside and end up at the park]* Well, I assume you wanted to have some 'man to man' talk?

Pat: Yes. As you know, Andrew is a good friend of the family, so, even though we told him he couldn't court Maydyn he is still over at our house all the time, and between him and Maydyn I have been hearing quite a bit about all of the discussions you have been having.
I was confident, a while ago, that what I was teaching was Scriptural. I had read a lot of courtship advocates: Bill Gothard, Douglas Wilson... and much of it seemed to make sense, and follow what Scripture taught. But now, well, I have been re-thinking.

Sakal: Always a good thing.

Pat: Well, yes, but, it's not exactly making my life easy. All this time I have been thinking of all of these wonderful qualifications that a potential 'suitor' must meet, and now I'm not sure what I'm supposed to be looking for!

Sakal: I understand. I think a large part of the church is just as confused, if not more so. But, in the end, you did decide to turn Andrew down?

Pat: Well, no, not really. It seems like forever ago that I told him he couldn't court Maydyn.

Sakal: And, why was that, anyway?

Pat: Well, since it is just the two of us, I guess I can tell you. You see, I'm not completely convinced about his thought life.

Sakal: Oh?

Pat: It seems to me that he is a bit *too* eager to get married, if you see what I mean.

Sakal: No, I can't say I do.

Pat: I don't want to malign a Godly young man but, well, I am not sure he has completely conquered lust.

Sakal: No, I doubt he has.

Pat: *[Sighs]* So you see it too? So you see why I can't let him court Maydyn?

Sakal: No.

Pat: You would let someone court one of your daughters who hadn't conquered lust?

Sakal: Leaving aside the question of courtship… I would certainly let a young man who hadn't conquered lust *marry* my daughter. In fact, quite the opposite… I don't think I would be inclined to let a young man who *had* conquered lust marry one of my daughters. We are looking forward to grandchildren…

Pat: I don't mean that! I don't mean he is a eunuch[cxxxiii]… spiritual or otherwise.

Sakal: Perhaps I misunderstood you. I thought you were saying that you wouldn't let a young man who was struggling with mental fornication… one who, when he looked at a beautiful young woman, was tempted to undress her with his eyes… that I wouldn't let someone like *that* marry my daughter.

Pat: That is what I mean! I wouldn't let him in my house!

Sakal: Then you had better keep Andrew out.

Pat: What?

Sakal: Let me put it this way: I want to give my daughter to a young man who will bless him, sexually. You remember Proverbs five?

Pat: Well, I think so...

Sakal: It reads like this: Proverbs 5:15-19 *Drink waters out of thine own cistern, and running waters out of thine own well. Let thy fountains be dispersed abroad, and rivers of waters in the streets. Let them be only thine own, and not strangers' with thee. Let thy fountain be blessed: and rejoice with the wife of thy youth. Let her be as the loving hind and pleasant roe; let her breasts satisfy thee at all times; and be thou ravished always with her love.*
I want to give my daughter to a man who will find this easy! I want to give her to someone for whom she will be a blessing.

Pat: Wow. But what about, I mean... don't you want her to be happy?

Sakal: Of course, but that is not my primary goal. Happiness is like health: if you make it your primary goal you end up sick. It is precisely when we stop focusing on her happiness, and focus instead on what she should be doing, what her God given goals are, that she will arrive at the happiness God has for her.
I want my daughter's goal to be to glorify God. And in marriage, I want her primary goal to be to be a blessing to her husband, to glorify God in that way. When a young man comes for my daughter... or when his father comes presenting him, I want my primary thought to be, "Can my daughter serve God by serving this man? Does she have what *he* needs?" We see in I Peter 3 a wife blessing a man who 'obeys not the word'. Our daughters do not serve God merely by marrying the best man in all the world, the most Godly man on the planet; they do it by marrying the man that needs her, the one God has created her for.

Pat: And the young man's father, should he be thinking the same thing?

Sakal: Well, sort of. The young man's father will, I hope, be thinking, "Will this young woman be able to meet my son's needs. Will she be able to bless him sexually and in every other way; and will their union meet our family goals of glorifying God?"

Pat: That, that's not what I meant! I meant, should the young man's father be thinking about how his son can bless his wife?

Sakal: That should be what he has trained him for, but it isn't what he should choose her for. She is being chosen as his helpmeet, not vice versa. I happen to believe that God has made women, in general, to be good helpmeets. I don't think that there are any such things, in the end, as bad matches[cxxxiv]. A father should be looking for the best wife for his son, the one with the most strengths etc.
But I don't think that should be the girl's father's goal. I see Scripture as

saying that his goal should be to answer the question, "is my daughter equipped to be a helpmeet to this young man, to bless him all of his days?"

As fathers of sons, we are to train our sons to love their wives, to give honor to them as the weaker vessel, and to guide them spiritually. But that is simply what we have trained them to do, it doesn't affect which particular girl they are to marry.

Pat: But... that seems so...

Sakal: Unequal? Foreign? Patriarchal?

Pat: Well, yes; which, with my knowledge of the Scriptures, should almost be a recommendation. Isn't that precisely the battle that the church is having in our generation: that we are finding so much of what Scripture tells us to do 'unequal, foreign, and patriarchal'?

Returning to our original subject, you are saying that almost all of our young men are, well, let's say 'healthy'. Some of them are more tempted, sexually, than others; and some have fallen farther than others in that area, but that God calls for all of them to get married.

Sakal: And I Corinthians 7 was written to the church. So they are to find their wives within the church... both the 'incontinent' young man and the young man who, while remaining much more pure, still wants a wife; both of them are to find their wives within the church. Both of them are to be able to come to you and say, "I need a wife."

And that need, while it must include all of the wonderful spiritual reasons for getting a wife: getting a helpmeet, growing toward being an elder or deacon, being fruitful... it should also be the spiritual need of avoiding fornication. Even if the young man, or his father, is not bold enough to state it, he is still allowed, indeed commanded, to need to rejoice in her physically and thus avoid the 'strange woman'.

Pat: That is a hard statement. Almost no one is saying that nowadays. They are all standing up in meetings, promoting books: and talking about all the things a young man has to be before he can marry... and the same for the young woman.

One very important scholar, very respected, has said that while a young man should look for a young woman that meets Proverbs 31 and Titus 2, the young woman and her father should seek a man that fits Titus 1.[cxxxv]

Sakal: A *very* respected commentator. I listened to his tape the other day. I would ask you a question about that message. He gave it, I presume, to a large group of men and boys. In effect he gave it to 'the church'... he made the case that these principles should apply to every Christian marriage.

Do you think that, if you had been the speaker who had given that message, you would have felt comfortable, afterwards, standing up, reading I Corinthians 7:2 and 9, and saying that you believed in applying that? That that passage was still true, and valid, for all Christians?

Pat: Well, no.

Obviously if the young man has to meet Titus 1, and the young woman Titus 2 and Proverbs 31, we are not going to be marrying, or 'letting them marry', 'every man' and 'every woman'; let alone the ones who are having the problem of I Corinthians 7:2 and 9! Not when they are young and struggling, anyway. Indeed the Titus qualification of 'blameless' seems to specifically contradict the I Corinthians 7 issue of 'cannot contain'. How can that pastor say of any man that 'cannot contain', or who is 'burning' that he is, at the same time, 'blameless'?

But, what he is saying is what practically all the modern commentators are saying, in one form or the other!

Sakal: Yet none of the old commentators say the same thing. I have the commentaries at home if you would like to look them up with me…

Pat: No, I don't mean to say I don't believe you, I just find it incredible that any Godly man would say such a thing; that any father could consider deliberately giving his daughter to a young man…

Sakal: Who was eager for the pleasures of the marriage bed? Were *you* not eager? Did *you* have lust conquered?

Pat: *[After a long period of silence]* Well, we are both married men, I suppose I can tell you that I did *not* have lust conquered. Indeed, Maydyn's mother and I… we… well, we came *pretty* close to having Maydyn less than nine months after our wedding.

Sakal: So you think that you should have waited until you had gotten lust conquered? Do you know of any young man that has lust conquered?

Pat: Well, certainly no young man that *I* actually know. But, how can I have some young man court my daughter if he, if they…

Sakal: Court? I didn't say anything about anyone *courting* one of my daughters. But the young man who *marries* my daughter, do I want him to want to sleep with her? Isn't that part of what marriage is about? Is it not written: *Let thy fountain be blessed: and rejoice with the wife of thy youth. Let her be as the loving hind and pleasant roe; let her breasts satisfy thee at all times; and be thou ravished always with her love.*[cxxxvi]

Pat: But that is once you already *have* a wife!

Sakal: Exactly.

I can certainly understand why you don't want them hanging around each other before they are in covenant together, but why not let them marry?

Pat: But how do they *get there*?!

I don't have anything against marriage, far from it. I would love for Maydyn to be married and bringing me grandchildren. I thought about what you said, or at least what part of it I heard, and what your wife said, and I was thinking about it. Maybe she *is* ready to be married. Maybe *they* are ready to be married. But how do we get there?

Sakal: Speaking of 'getting there', our walk has brought us full circle and we have arrived back at our house. Do you think that Andrew and Maydyn might want to be with us for the next part of this discussion? Are we done with the 'married men' part?

Pat: Sure.

XIV: The Joint Problem.

Sakal, Pat, Maydyn, and Andrew are all sitting at the kitchen table, with the noise of children in the background.

Pat: So, let me resume our discussion. Mr. Davidson and I were talking about some of the problems with having... *healthy* young men and women hang out together during courtship. He challenged me, and he was right, that I was a *healthy* young man when I dated... and that is one reason why I was so impressed with courtship. But if, umm, healthy young men and women are to get married, then, somehow, they need to get together. And, right now, I am rather frustrated with the current system... as, it seems, you two are.
Mr. Davidson and I had gotten to that part of our conversation, when we made it back here, and decided to invite the two of you to join us. It seems, from what I have seen, that there are a lot of problems with courtship, problems I thought we had left behind in dating. It seems that courtship works toward solving some issues, but not fully, and not Biblically. And we aren't getting our children married.

Sakal: We do seem to keep coming back to the same issues. That, no matter how much you try to differentiate them, there is something at the core of both dating and courtship that is the same, and that is wrong, very wrong. I think a good part of what's wrong with both dating and courtship are the 'dates'; the 'going out together'.

Andrew: What?!

Maydyn: What?

Pat: What?

Sakal: I'm not saying it is the *only* thing wrong, but it certainly seems to be one of them. My wife and I have done quite a study, along with all of you. We have examined Christian Dating, and all sorts of varieties of courtship... from the informal to the formal, the loose to the tightly chaperoned. And all of them seem to founder on this same rock, the rock of 'going out' or 'courting'. The young man and the young woman are encouraged into a series of encounters, which lead them to bind their hearts together, to various degrees... all of which are inappropriate, all of which encourage the young man to treat his sister in the Lord as something else, something more like a wife.

Andrew: But you can't get married without *dating*!

Maydyn: I wouldn't want to marry a boy who hadn't *courted* me.

Pat: How are they supposed to know if they are supposed to get married?

Sakal: That is a good question. How do you read it? What do the Scriptures say?

Pat: They don't! That's the whole problem! The Scriptures don't tell us how the boy and the girl are supposed to figure out who to marry!

Sakal: Oh? Let us see. Let's look at the Scriptures. They are full of *examples* of marriage, anyway. Let's start at the beginning. How did Adam know who he was supposed to marry?

Andrew: That was easy! God brought Eve to him.[cxxxvii]

Sakal: And how did Eve know who she was supposed to marry?

Maydyn: That was easy too, God brought her to Adam.

Sakal: How about Isaac?

Andrew: He had it easy, too. His father sent a servant to get him a wife. All he had to do was to take her into his tent.[cxxxviii]

Maydyn: But I don't know how Rebecca decided if she should marry Isaac.

Pat: She didn't, her father did. You remember, darling, how the servant came to her father and he, along with her brother, said, *The thing proceedeth from the LORD: we cannot speak unto thee bad or good. Behold, Rebekah is before thee, take her, and go, and let her be thy master's son's wife, as the LORD hath spoken.* [cxxxix]

Maydyn: But, later on, they asked her if she wanted to marry Isaac, didn't they?

Pat: No, not really, you remember the mother and the servant were having an argument about whether Rebecca and Abraham's servant should leave right away or after a few days and that was when they called her in and asked her if she 'would go'.

Maydyn: So she went because her father *told her* she should go?

Pat: Yes, that's the way I read it.

Maydyn: Oh.

Sakal: And how did Jacob know who he should marry?[cxl]

Andrew: That was harder. His father sent him off to the 'old country' to his mother's family to get a wife.

Sakal: But how did he know which wife to pick?

Andrew: Well, if I remember right, no, let me look it up: Genesis 28: 1-5 *And Isaac called Jacob, and blessed him, and charged him, and said unto him, Thou shalt not take a wife of the daughters of Canaan. Arise, go to Padanaram, to the house of Bethuel thy mother's father; and take thee a* *wife from thence of the daughters of Laban thy mother's brother. And God Almighty bless thee, and make thee fruitful, and multiply thee, that thou mayest be a multitude of people; And give thee the blessing of Abraham, to thee, and to thy seed with thee; that thou mayest inherit the land wherein thou art a stranger, which God gave unto Abraham. And Isaac sent away Jacob: and he went to Padanaram unto Laban, son of Bethuel the Syrian, the brother of Rebekah, Jacob's and Esau's mother.*

Genesis 29: 9-19 ... And it came to pass, when Jacob saw Rachel the daughter of Laban his mother's brother, and the sheep of Laban his mother's brother, that Jacob went near, and rolled the stone from the well's mouth, and watered the flock of Laban his mother's brother. And Jacob kissed Rachel, and lifted up his voice, and wept.

And Jacob told Rachel that he was her father's brother, and that he was Rebekah's son: and she ran and told her father. And it came to pass, when Laban heard the tidings of Jacob his sister's son, that he ran to meet him, and embraced him, and kissed him, and brought him to his house. And he told Laban all these things. And Laban said to him, Surely thou art my bone and my flesh. And he abode with him the space of a month.

And Laban said unto Jacob, Because thou art my brother, shouldest thou therefore serve me for nought? tell me, what shall thy wages be? And Laban had two daughters the name of the elder was Leah, and the name of the younger was Rachel. Leah was tender eyed; but Rachel was beautiful and well favoured. And Jacob loved Rachel; and said, I will serve thee seven years for Rachel thy younger daughter.

And Laban said, It is better that I give her to thee, than that I should give her to another man: abide with me."

So, anyway, his father sent him to that family and told him to marry one of the girls, and he picked the pretty one.

Sakal: And he married her?

Andrew: Well, sort of. He married the ugly one first…

Maydyn: Andrew! The Bible doesn't say she was *ugly*!

Andrew: Well, it says she was 'tender eyed' and I always thought that meant she was, you know, that she had something wrong with her face.

Maydyn: Andrew!

Andrew: *[Blushing]* Anyway, he married Leah first, and then Rachel, and then the two slave girls.

Sakal: But how did he know he was supposed to marry them?

Andrew: It doesn't really say. Rachel he married because his father said so, and she was pretty, and because her father said he could. Leah he married because her father slipped her into his honeymoon tent, and then he talked him into keeping her… and because *his* father said so too, I guess, she *was* one of the daughters of Laban. And then the two slave girls, his wives talked him into taking them.

Pat: Surely you aren't suggesting that we imitate the method of Jacob?

Andrew: Isn't it written that, *'All Scripture is given by inspiration of God, and is profitable for doctrine, for reproof, for correction, for instruction in righteousness: That the man of God may be perfect, thoroughly furnished unto all good works.'?*[cxli] Surely God must have put the story of Jacob in the Bible for a reason.

Pat: Perhaps it is to show us what *not* to do.

Sakal: Perhaps. But you will recall that we began this conversation to determine whether or not it was true that the Scriptures say *nothing at all* about the path to marriage. Even a 'don't do that' would still be saying something. Shall we keep looking?

Pat: Sure, yeah.

Sakal: So Maydyn, those girls, how did they know whether to marry Jacob?

Maydyn: Leah and Rachel married him because their father said so, and the two slave girls, well, they had to marry whoever their master told them to.

Sakal: Very well, who do we have left?

Maydyn: There's Ruth. She and Boaz courted!

Andrew: No, they didn't either. Here, let me read it to you… *Then Naomi her mother-in-law said unto her, My daughter, shall I not seek rest for thee, that it may be well with thee? And now is not Boaz of our kindred, with whose maidens thou wast? Behold, he winnoweth barley to night in the threshing floor. Wash thyself therefore, and anoint thee, and put thy raiment upon thee, and get thee down to the floor: but make not thyself known unto the man, until he shall have done eating and drinking. And it shall be, when he lieth down, that thou shalt mark the place where he shall lie, and thou shalt go in, and uncover his feet, and lay thee down; and he will tell thee what thou shalt do.*
And she said unto her, All that thou sayest unto me I will do.[cxlii]

Maydyn: So, she married the man that her mother-in-law told her to?

Pat: Sort of, sweetheart, you see there was a law that determined who she had to marry[cxliii].

Maydyn: And she *had to* marry him?

Pat: Well, yes. You see Ruth although she was a Moabitess not a Jewess, had deliberately decided to obey God's law[cxliv]… including that one.

Maydyn: Wow! I never knew that.

Pat: We could go through the rest of the marriages, but it seems to me we are seeing a lot of similarity between these stories, and a lot of differences with ours. The problem that I see is that children of today wouldn't be willing to follow the Biblical pattern.

Andrew: Hey!

Maydyn: Daddy!

Pat: What, would you? Andrew, would you be willing to get married like Othniel[cxlv] or David[cxlvi]? If I set you some big challenge, something you had to go out and do, some enemy you had to conquer, would you do it?

Andrew: *[Puffing out his chest]* To marry Maydyn? Sure I would, if I could. There aren't a hundred Philistines around to kill nowadays but, what would it take?!

Pat: Ahem. Well, perhaps you would *[He glances at Sakal]*, but what of you, Maydyn? Would you marry Andrew just because he accomplished some task I set before him?

Maydyn: If he asked me.

Andrew: But that wasn't what happened in Scripture! The father set the task, and the boy did it, and the girl went along.

Maydyn: *[Looks at her father]* Yeah, I guess I would do that, too. If Daddy thought that was the right thing to do. I'm not sure this is a fair test, though, because I already know Andrew, we practically grew up together.

Pat: Yes, perhaps I asked the wrong thing. Andrew, what if your father called you into his office and talked about how he had picked this nice girl for you, and she would be arriving tomorrow with a friend of his…?

Andrew: *[After a pause]* I can't quite imagine my father doing that, but, you know, I think I would be OK with it, especially if it happened tomorrow. I would be, I suppose, a bit taken aback if it wasn't Maydyn…

Maydyn: And me, Daddy? Would you just pick someone for me?

Pat: No, because you have said that you wouldn't accept someone if I did that. Not that I had considered it before, but you have made that clear in the past.

Maydyn: I hadn't thought of it either! That doesn't mean I would *disobey* you!

Pat: But, you always said…

Maydyn: Because I thought that was *right!* That's what we always talked about; that's what I always thought I *would* do. I never read the story of Rebecca as if it could be *me!*

Andrew: I never thought I could be Isaac. I don't even know how to ride a camel! *[Everyone glares at him. He grins and lifts his hands. Sheepishly.]* Sorry!

Pat: But, if I pick a husband for my daughter, or a wife for my son, how am I supposed to know if they will be compatible; without their dating or courting or anything?

Andrew: *[Chuckles]*

Pat: What?

Andrew: I already asked that, and have been thinking a lot about the answer.

Pat: Well, what was the answer?

Andrew: First of all, and most importantly, it seems that God has made women to be compatible with men… or incompatible, depending on how you look at it; to be alike, but different; to be helpmeets. So *any* truly Godly woman will be a good helpmeet to *any* truly Godly man. Nowhere in Scripture is it written that there exists some 'index of compatibility' that the couple has to have; except their willingness to obey God and His commands about marriage.

Pat: OK, I can see that. What was your other reason?

Andrew: Well, the more I think about it, the more I am afraid we have it all backwards. If you had to choose between me and my father as far as picking the right wife for me, any person with intelligence would choose my father to do the deciding. He is older, has more wisdom, and is less… personally involved. *[Everyone stares at Andrew for a minute, who blushes.]*

Pat: I think I see what you mean. The young man or *[He looks at his daughter.]* young woman are apt to be driven by their hormones, and their standard of beauty or masculinity; whereas the father can be more objective, and dwell on more important issues.

Andrew: But, wait a minute. In our earlier conversation *[He looks at Sakal.]* we agreed that Scripture *didn't* list all sorts of requirements for a wife or husband?!

Pat: That doesn't mean that the father just goes out and grabs someone off the street.
It is a far different thing to go out and seek a wife for your son, and do the best you can for him, than having a checklist that the girl or boy must

meet or there is no marriage. Let us say, God forbid, that the two of you were to get in trouble and *need* to marry *[Maydyn and Andrew both blush crimson]*. A checklist would imply that I should refuse... since Andrew has obviously demonstrated that he is not 'up to snuff' as far as the checklist is concerned[cxlvii]. But Scripture, both in the law[cxlviii] and the New Testament,[cxlix] insists the opposite.

The emphasis on the checklists of the courtship advocates don't seem to be on 'how can I get the best husband for my daughter, but 'how can I avoid getting an unworthy husband for my daughter.' The end result is not a series of perfect marriages, but a series of non-marriages... of older, unmarried daughters and sons.

Abraham sent his servant out with a checklist, but the emphasis was on finding the wife, and he found one. His checklist was simple, and objective: a daughter of my people, not a Canaanite, and Isaac wasn't to go down there to get her. And the servant found a wife, and right away. But the modern checklists are miles long: Finances, education, doctrine... I have heard of dozens of courtships that foundered on one or another of these rocks... or simply the undefined disapproval of one of the parties. And the people on the other end, the sons or the father's of sons, have no idea what was involved in the checklist. In the end, we are left with marriages which are either delayed or denied altogether.

Pat: *[Looks at Sakal]* I would like to talk to you more about this, later.

XV: Gaining Oneness.

Later in the evening Pat and Sakal are sitting at the kitchen table. The women's voices can be heard, quietly, in the background.

Pat: I had another question.

Sakal: Yes?

Pat: One of the most important things I have been reading about in the whole courtship issue is the idea of oneness.[cl] Most everything that I've read talks about how the couple needs to start becoming one during the courtship period. Some people talk about mental oneness, some about spiritual oneness.

Sakal: And the physical?

Pat: Oh, no. That has to wait for marriage itself.

Sakal: I see. So the idea is that you move through these stages, becoming more and more one, until finally you start sleeping together?

Pat: Well, no one would put it quite *that* way.

Sakal: I suppose not. But what about you; what do you think?

Pat: Well, the idea of a growing oneness resonates with me. It's rather similar to what my wife and I did.

Sakal: Yes, it *is* very similar to the dating model.

Pat: Ouch. *[A long pause]* You mean that in courtship they end up forming a relationship that, if eventually broken off, was inappropriate? We talk about them being 'one flesh' and we use that as a euphemism for marital intimacy, but we also want it to mean more than that. We want her to be a helpmeet.[cli] We want them to have common goals, and to have learned to work well together.

Sakal: Yet we don't want that...

Pat: Outside of marriage. Wow. It's true. I want my daughter to be fulfilling *my* goals, as her father, but only in preparation for her fulfilling her *husband's* goals once she is married.[clii]

Sakal: And you don't want her working on *some other man's goals* in the meantime.

Pat: No, I don't. I didn't think of that before. Is there any way to avoid that conflict?

Sakal: Other than by *not* having them date or court? How?
Both dating and courting require forming a relationship... and the kind of

relationship they form must, of necessity, be 'marriage lite'. They aren't meeting to collect stamps or solve world hunger through political action: they are coming together as a boy and a girl on the road to marriage. It seems to me that all of the things that dating and courtship advocates say they *want* to happen during the dating and courting time are the very things that, if the dating or courting doesn't work out, are things that, in hindsight, they *didn't* want to have happened... things that need to be undone by the next relationship, and that damage it. Two start becoming one, even if not physically, and then, if the courtship fails, you ask them to become two again; an impossible task.

Pat: Wow.

Sakal: Ironically, Scripture talks about such relationships, and every single one of them is negative.

Pat: Yes, I heard that list; Charles buttonholed me to talk about it. He was rather depressed.

Sakal: *[Chuckles, then sobers up.]* But there is another pertinent issue we need to recognize. Most courtship models say that the relationship is supposed to go through several phases.

Pat: Yes: Pre-friendship, friendship, courting, engagement, marriage.

Sakal: Yes. Now the 'oneness' of these stages is important, but I think there is something much more serious that we must look at. In each of these stages the individuals concerned make a sort of commitment, no?

Pat: What do you mean?

Sakal: Well, let us say that a young man, George, is thinking it is time for him to marry. So he looks around the church, among his friends, or whatever, and says, "I wonder who I should court?" He looks at a series of girls and says, "Should I court her?"
Well, even if he thinks about her for a minute or two, he has thought about her, as a possible wife.

Pat: And you're worried about his thought life?

Sakal: Well, that is an issue, but that isn't what I'm talking about now. Right now I'm talking about his 'commitment life'. For those few seconds, he has made a very small, very light, commitment to that girl.

Pat: Oh, I see. Even if just to say, "Thinking about her as my wife for a second here..."

Sakal: Exactly. And then, when he, for whatever reason, decides she isn't right; he breaks off that commitment.

Pat: But, if he does decide to pursue it further, he 'commits' to thinking about her more seriously, and cultivates a friendship with her.

Sakal: Exactly, all the while thinking of her as a 'wife lite'. Then, a week, or a month, later, he decides she isn't exactly what he is looking for and, 'breaks it off'.

Pat: But, hopefully, he hasn't said anything to her.

Sakal: Very true. But then the day comes, when he has gone through all these steps, and finally asks the father for permission to court the daughter. Now his heart is even more committed.

Pat: Oh, my. I see where you are going. This is awful. From the time of pre-friendship, through courting, he has gotten used to making commitments and then, when the girl on the other end doesn't turn out to be what he was thinking, he drops her, he breaks that commitment. Then, when he comes to marry a girl, he has gotten into the horrible habit of making, then breaking commitments. But *surely* he will understand that the marriage commitment is one that can't be broken just because he finds a fault in the girl!

Sakal: Hopefully; but even if he does, what of his heart? Will he not, in his heart, carry about seeds of dissatisfaction; a hidden thought that it 'isn't fair' and 'I should be able to drop her'? Isn't that what all his previous experience has taught him?

Pat: Wow!... and our daughters as well, although in a different fashion. She would get used to having, and then losing... or even dropping... various boys. So even when she commits to marriage, she retains her old habits.

Sakal: In the end we can never prevent our children from forming harmful attachments. But surely we can do better than to put them in a system that guarantees them! That even encourages them!

Pat: Wow. Well, you've given me a whole lot to think about, as much as I can handle. Shall we rejoin our wives?

[The two get up from the table and walk out the kitchen door.]

XVI: Taking Initiative.

Sakal is sitting at a table in the park when a man walks up to him...

Abe: Sakal? Sakal Davidson? I'm Abe, Abe Adamson.

Sakal : *[Rising and shaking his hand]* I'm pleased to meet you. So, you're Andrew's father?

Abe: Yes, and you are Sakal, the man I have been hearing so much about. Our dinner conversations have been very animated recently.

Sakal: Sorry!

Abe: No, it's been good. I hadn't realized how much of our culture we had just accepted. Andrew came home and told me some people were talking about not dating and, after freaking out, I started looking into the issue myself... following from afar, as it were.

Sakal: ...and now you've come to confront me directly?

Abe: Confront? No, to thank you.

Sakal: Oh?

Abe: Yes. I haven't been challenged like this in years. The more I studied the Scriptures, the more issues I found; issues I had just taken for granted before. I would like to run some of my thoughts by you.

Sakal: Sure.

Abe: Starting at the beginning, it seems like the Scriptures are completely bereft of anything our culture would call 'dating' or 'courting'... any idea of the young man and the young woman pursuing a relationship together. All of the relationships, the best relationships at least, started with some form of covenant or agreement.

Sakal: Betrothal.

Abe: Yes, or espousal, when they translate it from the Greek, at least in the KJV. Before that they are supposed to only be brother and sister[cliii].

Sakal: An unpopular conclusion; and it points out a major problem with courtship, especially for our young men. They know, in their hearts, they are supposed to treat the young women as sisters. But courtship, if it is to work, forces them to go beyond that, to treat the young women as potential wives, *before* they are in covenant.
As a result, some of them, some of the best of them, don't court at all. They never get past the point of 'sister' to the point of 'future wife'... since they know they aren't supposed to think like that.

Abe: Wow, I never thought of it that way.
The second thing I discovered had to do with the timing of marriage. All of the passages point toward young marriages, *very* young marriages by our standards. God constantly speaks of the young couple being fertile, of having children. He talks about what a blessing a wife is to a man, a young man... a blessing that lasts all of his life. Anyway, all of these things helped convince me that I should get serious about Andrew and his ideas and plans.

Sakal: Why you?

Abe: A good question, although I have a feeling you know the answer. All of my life I've grown up with the idea that it was up to the kids to figure the whole thing out; but now I am seeing that *I* am supposed to be taking care of this issue, or, at least, taking the initiative.

Sakal: So, what are you going to do?

Abe: I'm going to go confront Pat with my problem.

Sakal: Good for you.

Abe: Or, rather, I'm going to ask you to go for me.

Sakal: Oh?

Abe: If you'll do it, I think it would be better. I'm new to all this and...well... don't know it very well. If well, if Maydyn's father starts to talk about a litany of things wrong with Andrew, I'm rather afraid I will just agree with him and walk away ashamed. I'm hoping you will be better suited to the job.

Sakal: Well, I will do my best. Andrew is fine *young* man. But I can't promise anything. The church is rather stuck in neutral on this issue... with people actually saying that the reason that the young people aren't getting married is because they 'aren't ready'[cliv] or because it isn't 'the Lord's will'.

Abe: You're not saying it is outside of the Lord's will?

Sakal: Yes and no. Everything that happens is according to the Lord's will, but that doesn't mean that everything we do is sinless. It was certainly the Lord's will that Pharaoh and his army were drowned in the Red Sea. But that doesn't mean that, if you had been one of his counselors, you wouldn't have advised him to take a slightly different tack in regards to the children of Israel.

Abe: *[Laughs]* No. No, you're right we need to be doing the right thing, the obedient thing, regardless. The Lord will work everything out for good, but *we* still need to do what is right, as well as we can.

Sakal: Exactly. So many people are just sitting, waiting, when they should be up and doing.

Abe: Speaking of which…

Sakal: Oh, right. Let me see, do you have their phone number? And I have a couple more questions for you…

XVII: A Confrontation.

Sakal and Pat come into a restaurant together, and, after they are seated...

Pat: So, what's up with the meeting, at a restaurant and all?

Sakal: I have something very important, and rather private, to discuss with you.

Pat: More about courtship and dating?

Sakal: Sort of. More about marriage.

Pat: Sounds interesting.

Sakal: Well, I certainly hope you will be interested. I am speaking about the marriage of Maydyn and Andrew.

Pat: *[After a long pause]* You're serious?

Sakal: Very.

Pat: Not dating, not courtship, just... marriage?

Sakal: Sort of. The actual stage would be called 'betrothal'; where they are bound in covenant together, but have not yet 'come together'.[clv]

Pat: This seems... I am... I am very surprised, in one sense, but in another, not really. Our conversation seems to have been leading inexorably in this direction. And, more and more, I am... not unwilling. What are you actually proposing?

Sakal: Well, Abe came to me the other day and we discussed it. He is of the opinion that Andrew needs a wife.

Pat: Like 'needs' as in...

Sakal: As in he is a *healthy* young man, and, besides, he is a healthy young *man*, and it is time for him to step up to the responsibilities of a husband and father.

Pat: Is he going to be able to afford an apartment, and insurance, and all of that?

Sakal: He won't need to. His parents have agreed there is really no reason he should have to move out of their house, even once he brings his wife home. His father said, "I don't have many mansions in my house, but I have an extra bedroom, anyway."[clvi]
He and his father, assuming you agree, will build a bathroom onto his bedroom, which should make living a little less tight, and give the new young couple a little more privacy. And he has a job, so insurance should be OK. Although his father *was* talking about wanting to bring him into the family business, and said that they could provide, regardless.

Pat: But what about 'leave and cleave'?

Sakal: What about it?

Pat: Doesn't it mean he needs his own apartment?

Sakal: Is that what you see in Scripture?

Pat: Well, no, I've always wondered about that. Almost none of the examples in Scripture show the young man 'going off' in any meaningful sense; even Abraham who 'left his father's house'. It seems to me that that example almost shows that he was expected to stay in his father's house, and indeed where he and his wife had been living, and that God was calling them to do something extraordinary by leaving. The rest of the patriarchs seemed to live with, and work with, their fathers, or their fathers-in-law.

Sakal: ...which used to be the norm for our cultures as well. The 'old country', England is full of houses that are so big as to be practically useless, because everyone goes off to live by themselves.

Pat: So, does this mean I will get a bride price too? (Chuckling)

Sakal: Yes. Abe is proposing ten thousand dollars.

Pat: What? I was kidding! I don't want to *sell* my daughter!

Sakal: No one wants you to. But the bride price plays a significant function; it shows her value. And the point isn't that you get the money but that you keep it for your daughter, if Andrew should ever abandon her.

Pat: Wow. This seems like something out of an old movie. But, is he really ready? It sounds like he doesn't really have his finances and all worked out. You know, "prepare your fields."[clvii]

Sakal: Yet another verse that everyone quotes though it has nothing to do with marriage.[clviii] If you believe he needs more time to be ready to bring your daughter home, then that is fine. I won't be happy (and Andrew *definitely* won't be happy) but that is your prerogative. But you need not hinder the betrothal. Just make their betrothal contingent on his earning so much money, or passing a test or something.

But I won't agree to any long conditions. The Jews had a tradition that the groom had one year to prepare the place he was going to bring his wife back to; in our sexually crazed society I think that is more than enough time, probably too much; for Andrew and Maydyn, in particular, the shorter the better.

Pat: I don't understand this 'conditional betrothal'.

Sakal: Well, perhaps it is hard to understand for us poor moderns. In the past, a betrothal could happen one of two ways. Either the fathers would agree, and the betrothal was immediately valid; or the bride's father would set some condition, like 'take this city', and there would be no betrothal until the city was taken.

On the other end, sometimes there was a payment that needed to be made, and until it was paid they were betrothed, but couldn't come together. Sometimes the young man's father would set him a task.

But in today's society, I think we need to be very careful. We are surrounded by rampant fornication. If we betroth someone very young, then it is just as well that they have to wait to come together, and that he have some task in the mean time. But if they are older, as so many of our children are, I think we need to simply 'let them marry'.

Pat: So, what else?

Sakal: Abe already talked to Andrew, and Andrew has agreed to marry whomever his father picks. I'm sure he is suspicious, and hopeful, that it is Maydyn, but he doesn't *know*.

Pat: Well, Maydyn already told me the same thing. We had a long talk, as a family, after you and I talked last. To my utter amazement my wife and all of my children said that, if I thought it was right, I could pick their spouses... for my children...

Sakal: *[Grins]* Yes, your wife already is married, and to a fine husband.

Pat: A humiliated husband, really. I had so little confidence in them, and so little confidence in myself.

[A pause and then he continues]... and Abe sent *you* to ask me?

Sakal: Yes.

Our society is not very good at this; we are out of practice. If you needed to turn Andrew down, he figured it would be easier if you weren't face to face, as it were. I can more forcefully argue Andrew's qualities, without any need for modesty, since he is not my son. He also gave me the authority to go to another father, if you *do* turn Andrew down.

Pat: Well, I'm not going to.

Looking back, I have let this relationship go far, far too far if I was going to turn him down. My wife and I were talking about this and we realized what we had allowed to happen. Andrew has already told Maydyn that she is 'the only girl he knew that he would consider marrying'. He asked her out on a date, and she was eager to start courting him. He has been hanging around our house ever since... I am afraid her heart is already partially committed, and I know he is eager for her... and much of that is my fault. I blew a very uncertain trumpet[clix], and they responded as well as they could.

But, tell me more about the betrothal period. I understand betrothal is a binding commitment, and a permanent one. We read through Ephesians five the other night and I was amazed, again, at how many times I had read that passage and not realized that it spoke of our betrothal to Christ, as a church.

But, as a practical matter, how long do you expect this period to last, before they 'come together'?

Sakal: That is up to two people:

First of all, you. As we said, if you wish, you can set a time limit, or some condition, and the betrothal wouldn't be fully effective till then.

Pat: And the other person?

Sakal: Andrew. Under the direction of his father, he will decide when to come for his bride.

Pat: So, like, ten minutes after I say it's OK?

Sakal: *[Grins]*

XVIII: You Can't do that!

Sakal is sitting at the park table, his lunch finished, his legs up, reading a book when an older man, conservatively dressed, comes up to him.

George: Sakal? Sakal Davidson?

Sakal: Yes? [Sakal gets up, the two shake hands, then they sit down across from each other.]

George: I'm George, George Wakefield; Senior Pastor at First Baptist here in town. I have heard that you have been having a series of discussions on the issue of courtship.

Sakal: That's right. Are you interested in the subject?

George: Well, yes. But I am even more interested in the hermeneutic you are using to arrive at your, shall we say, unorthodox conclusions.

Sakal: Well, I wouldn't call them unorthodox… but I am also interested in discussing hermeneutics; and would love to talk about it.

George: Well, good. Now, I have heard a lot of the issues you have raised, and the problem I see with your hermeneutic, is that you seem to see things which are merely stories, or merely statements about the culture of Bible times, as commands.

Sakal: I see. So, what would you have me do?

George: Well, we need to separate those things which are clearly commands, from those which aren't.

Sakal: Then what do we do?

George: I'm sorry?

Sakal: Once we have selected those things which are clearly commands, and eliminated the rest of Scripture, what are we to do? Specifically in this area, there are no commands which say 'thou shalt betroth', or 'thou shalt court, or date'. How then shall our children be married?

George: I don't... well, that means we are free to do it however we feel is best.

Sakal: Hopefully you don't really mean as we '*feel*' is best. But how, then, do we determine what is right, if we eliminate Scripture?

George: I'm not saying we should eliminate Scripture!

Sakal: So, then, tell me, how do you apply Scripture to this problem? How do we determine what the best thing to do is? My theology, my *hermeneutic,* if you will, teaches me that the only place to look for the 'best' thing to do, is in Scripture.

George: Well, of course.

Sakal: And it teaches me that *"All Scripture is given by inspiration of God, and is profitable for doctrine, for reproof, for correction, for instruction in righteousness: That the man of God may be perfect, thoroughly furnished unto all good works."*[clx]

George: Yes.

Sakal: Then, it is not merely the commands that are profitable for doctrine. God gave the examples of the patriarchs, the Psalms, the Proverbs, even the actual language of the Scriptures as profitable for us.

George: Yes... but...

Sakal: Yes?

George: It isn't like Scripture tells us everything about *everything*!

Sakal: No, but it is 'sufficient' for the man of God, to be perfect, to be complete: to serve God. And if it is sufficient for that, then it is sufficient for this part of our lives.
Let me ask you, when you read a book on courtship, what do you look for? Things that sound wise? Or things that come from Scripture?

George: Things that come from Scripture.

Sakal: So, in order to determine what is best, we have to compare... compare courtship against Scripture. And find what Scripture really says about the various principles.

George: That's what we do.

Sakal: And we need to be prepared when we find that the courtship principles are not supported in Scripture, but something else is.

George: Well, I can't believe that you think the principles you are espousing are found in Scripture. I have heard that you think fornicators should be allowed to marry!

Sakal: Well, it was Paul's idea, not mine.

George: Well, they can't marry *my* daughter.

Sakal: That seems to be the attitude of most of the courtship advocates. The 'Not My Daughter' Syndrome'. I see at least two major problems with that...

George: Oh?

Sakal: The first is that it seems to directly contradict I Corinthians 7. In that passage Paul keeps saying 'let them marry'. Now, the way that translates into English is interesting; and meaningful. The underlying form is, of course, a kind of a command, like 'let us pray'... which means 'pray now!'
But the English form comes out very interestingly, basically as a command for those who might stop something, to *stop* stopping it. It means 'Let them' marry. Allow them to marry.
So this verse should, in my opinion, be treated as a dual command. For the young man and woman, it is a command to marry. To the people surrounding them, the church, their parents, their culture, it is a command to 'let them marry'. It says, "Get out of the way, stop creating obstacles, live up to your responsibilities and 'let them marry'".

George: Well, let them, but not my daughter.

Sakal: Or anyone else's, if the courtship advocates would have their way; which is my point. Remember what James said about sending the naked and hungry person away saying 'be warmed and filled'?[clxi] A 'not my daughter' attitude, consistently applied, is exactly the same.
God lists a wife as a need of a young man, a need just as important as food or clothing; a blessing and a gift worth far more than rubies. And yet our courtship advocates are sending young men away rejected, and with no real prospect for meeting their need. In the end the young man doesn't get married, or get's married far later than we would wish... as does the daughter.

George: What?

Sakal: That seems to be the result. So many obstacles have been created that, in the end, our daughters aren't marrying...and the most 'perfect' daughters seem to marry the latest, if at all. What good is raising a perfect daughter if she is never allowed to be a wife?
And it is illogical. If your daughter, your particular daughter, is really the absolute cream of the crop, and stands head and shoulders above the rest in purity, chastity, love, and obedience... then maybe it is precisely

the *least* qualified young man that she should marry, in order to be the most help for him. We set the best doctors to the hardest cases, do we not?

Voddie Baucham wrote a book, "What he must be to marry my daughter." Perhaps you should write a book, "What he will be *because* he marries my daughter."

Who in Scripture would you have considered worthy to marry your daughter? Paul, the murderer? David, the adulterer? Peter, the betrayer? Paul says, "Let every man have his own wife." Every man. Every single man.

He wrote his letter to the church at Corinth, and said they needed to see to it that every single man, and woman, in their church should be married: those that were struggling with fornication, those that were not yet struggling with fornication but might be soon, and those who merely wished for a wife... that they each should 'marry and not burn'. Elsewhere, he denounced 'forbidding to marry'.[clxii]

George: But I haven't trained my daughter to marry a fornicator!

Sakal: Why not? I have. I have trained my daughter the way an army trains its new recruits... for a battle, not a vacation. I have no idea what difficulties she might face in marriage: an unGodly husband, life on a mission field, barrenness, even abandonment. So my job is to train her for the worst possible scenario, the hardest possible situation.

Look at the women of Scripture, the truly Godly women in Scripture. Which of them married the perfect man and had the perfect life? Esther, who became part of a pagan king's harem? Mary, who was always known as a fornicator? One of the many wives of David?

It seems to me that you are seeking a life for your daughter that God hasn't called her to, and rejecting God's commands: for her and for you.

George: Those are horrible comparisons! I want my daughter to have a happy life!

Sakal: But maybe that isn't God's highest priority. I Corinthians 7, and I Peter 3, both speak of daughters married to unGodly men, and both show them blessing their husbands. None of us want our daughters to marry such men. We all dream of them having the perfect, fairy tale, marriage. But none of our marriages are like that. And in our quest for the perfect, we are missing not only the good, but God's commands. And it is our obedience to those commands, not the perfection of the to-be-married couple, that will lead to the 'perfect' marriage.

George: Obviously you haven't read what the church is beginning to say about a 'multi-generational vision'.[clxiii]

Sakal: But I have. And much of it is very Godly.

George: Well, then, how can you justify what you are saying? If a young man is going to fit into my multi-generational vision, he needs to be much more than a mere Christian... and much more than merely free of lustful thoughts. He must have qualities that fit him for my vision, qualities that raise him to the level of an elder, or a deacon at least.[clxiv]

Sakal: There is a quality I think you are missing...that much of the courtship crowd is missing.

George: Oh? What is that?

Sakal: He must exist!
Many of the 'multi-generational' advocates wrote their plans with the assumption that their sons and daughters would be married at an early age. But they aren't married. They aren't marrying. Their fathers may have done excellent work in writing up the plan, but they haven't done so well at the whole 'take wives for your sons' thing, and they are even worse at obeying the command to 'give your daughters in marriage'.[clxv] It seems these men have multiplied their requirements for the wives of their sons, or the husbands of their daughters, and forgotten the most basic requirement: they must exist, and be available, at the right time.[clxvi]

Andrew: *[Coming over to the table with Maydyn in hand]* Pastor! Mr. Davidson! *[Everyone rises and greets each other]* What's up?

George: *[Looking curiously at Maydyn]* Oh, we were having a discussion on hermeneutics; among other things.

Andrew: How interesting. If I know Mr. Davidson, you were being challenged!

George: I wouldn't put it quite like that. We were having some differences. But, you will have to excuse me, I know you, Andrew, from that year you came to our youth camp, but I don't think this young lady and I have met before.

Andrew: *[Grinning hugely]* Ah, well, this is my wife Maydyn, my betrothed wife.

George: *[Shocked]* Your wife?! I had no idea! I must have missed the wedding announcement.

Andrew: Oh, we haven't had our *wedding* yet, just our betrothal.

George: *[Looking back and forth from Sakal to Andrew]* Then why do you call her your wife?

Andrew: *[Squeezing her hand]* Because she is. Just like Mary was Joseph's *wife*, and the church is the *wife* of Christ.

George: That's entirely different.

Andrew: *[With a sidelong grin at Sakal]* Oh, why?

George: We... we don't do that anymore.

Andrew: *[Squeezing Maydyn's hand again]* We did!

George: But, you can't call her your wife, people will be confused.

Andrew: I think people are already confused, with all of this 'fiancée' stuff. Confused and nervous. I know I would be.

George: Really, why?

Andrew: Well, with a fiancée, you are always wondering, "Will she back out of our engagement?" But with Maydyn, she's my *wife*!

George: No, not really. You haven't been married, you know.

Andrew: Well, I haven't taken her home yet, but we are in covenant.

George: Oh, you mean... you mean you actually have your marriage license, and a pastor has performed a ceremony? Why then do you say you haven't married her yet?

Andrew: No, we haven't done any of that, we aren't *going* to do any of that. But even without that we are in covenant. Her father gave her to me. *[He looks lovingly at Maydyn, who grins at him and squeezes his hand.]*

George: But, but, you *have* to do those things! You can't just sleep with her!

Andrew: I can *now*, she's my wife. But we are going to wait a week or so, we have some details to work out regarding the celebration and honeymoon. Maydyn, well, she's a woman, and she wants a celebration.

George: Oh, I misunderstood you then. I thought you were not going to have a wedding. Who is going to perform the ceremony and make you man and wife?

Andrew: I told you, Maydyn's father already 'performed' it. He took her hand, placed it in mine, and said, "Take her, and let her be your wife." Happiest moment of my life!

Maydyn: *[Leaning against him]* And mine.

George: But that's not right! Somebody has to pronounce you man and wife at the *wedding*!

Andrew: Oh? That's not what we find in Scripture. A wedding is a celebration of a covenant already made.

George: That's just crazy. Nobody is doing that nowadays!

Andrew: *[Decisively]* We are!

George: But... well, I suppose that is something else we will talk about. Congratulations. How long did you court?

Andrew: *[Grinning]* We didn't. Her dad wouldn't let me court her.

George: *[Looking shocked]* Then how did you... you didn't...?!

Andrew: Sleep with her? No, sir! Her dad gave her to me. Her dad and my dad talked and they decided we should marry, and then they told us.

George: You mean, "Asked you."

Andrew: Nope, 'told us'. It was so funny. My dad came to me, sat me down, and started out, "Andrew, as you know you are getting older..." and I interrupted him. "Who is she?" I asked.
And he blushed, sort of, and said it was Maydyn. And you should have heard me scream with joy. I was prepared, in case it was someone else, but I had, foolishly, allowed my thoughts and actions to already turn toward Maydyn.

George: I'm glad he chose someone you could appreciate. And you, Maydyn, how did your father ask you?"

Maydyn: My father didn't 'ask' me either, he told me...

George: What?! He forced you to marry Andrew?

Maydyn: It wasn't force. He came to me a couple of days before and we had a long talk, our whole family did. Dad explained to us everything Scripture says about how to get married. I knew what was coming, of course, but the other kids hadn't heard so much. It was good to hear it all laid out.
He explained how, if we would let him, he would pick out spouses for us... in conjunction, that is, with the father of the other boy or girl involved. I said 'yes' right away, and my siblings followed suit, after a few questions. Joseph, my oldest brother, was particularly interested in 'when'... and rather excited by my dad's answer.

George: How can you not call that force? He picked your husband for you! You seem very happy with him, and that is fine, but the principle that you two seem to be espousing is, at its root, a form of force!

Andrew: Have you ever given your children gifts?

George: Of course.

Andrew: Was that force? Or do you always have your children pick their own gifts?

George: What?

Andrew: My father gave me a gift, the gift of a wife. Maydyn's father gave it with him. He worked year after year preparing a wife for me, and then, one day, he gave her to me. How is that force? Now, as for Maydyn...

Maydyn: ...As for Maydyn, her father gave her a gift, the gift of a husband!

XIX: Interlude

As I trotted my horse down the road I saw before me a marvelous sight; a garden[clxvii] enclosed by high, strong walls[clxviii]. A beautiful silver palace sat in the midst of the garden[clxix]. The garden had a spring[clxx], sending out streams of clear water[clxxi], watering plants, myriads of plants[clxxii].

I saw lilies[clxxiii] and pomegranates[clxxiv] in the garden; palm trees[clxxv] and nut trees[clxxvi]. Even from where I rode, coming down the hill toward the garden, I could smell the most marvelous smells coming over the walls: spikenard and saffron; calamus and cinnamon, with all trees of frankincense; myrrh and aloes, with all the chief spices[clxxvii].

As I rode closer, I saw another sight, as impressive in its own way. On the ramparts of the castle, splendidly arranged in armor, were several young men, marching to and fro, and keeping a vigilant eye in every direction. I saw that they had already seen me and were keeping a wary eye on me.[clxxviii]

My road led me to the front gate, where I saw another man, an older man, in well-used armor[clxxix]. He was standing in front of a gate, a well locked gate, all made of thick, strong planks of cedar.

The man smiled at me as I rode up and said, "Welcome, brother. Come and rest yourself." He waved his hand and I saw, standing beside the gate, a table. Even as I stopped a young boy came forward to hold the reins of my horse and an older woman and several younger women came to the table, setting it for a meal, all unspeaking.

"I thank you all for your courtesy," I said, "but I have business that cannot brook delay."[clxxx]

"What, then, is your business?" the man asked.

"I come on behalf of another," I said, "a young man under my command. He begins to thirst, and hunger[clxxxi], and I seek a garden for him."

"Is he a loyal son?" the man asked, "to you and to our common Lord?"

"He is…" I said, but just as I spoke one of the young warriors called, out.

"My lord, another man comes."

We both looked up to see a young man come riding up. "Welcome," the lord said, and the young man leapt from his horse. "Refresh yourself."

The young man, pleased, went to the table and helped himself to the food and wine. The lord and I exchanged glances, and then he said, "Tell me, what is your business here?"[clxxxii]

The young man flushed and said, "I would have your leave to talk to the lady of this garden."

The lord's eyes chilled slightly, "I am the lord of this garden, what words would you have with her?"[clxxxiii]

"You are its lord?" he asked, "I had understood that it was without a lord, that no one drank of its waters."

"I am the lord of the garden, but I do not drink of its waters. I and mine are charged with guarding it until the day comes when I give the charge of it to another."[clxxxiv]

"You give it? Must not the lady herself give it?"

"The lady? She is under my authority. How can she appoint her own lord? How can the lesser appoint the greater?"[clxxxv]

"With your blessing!"

"My blessing?" the lord said, very coldly. But then he softened, perhaps remembering the foolish young man he had once been. "Tell me, my son, are you thirsty?"[clxxxvi]

The young man, having a cup of wine in his hand paused and glanced at it, then, realizing that the question had nothing to do with wine, he flushed, "I... no!"

"Then you have no need of a garden, my son,"[clxxxvii] the lord turned back to me. "The young man you represent, he hungers and thirsts?"

"Yes."

"And you understand the value of this, my garden?"[clxxxviii]

I said I did, and together we discussed what price would be paid. Then, agreed, we sat together. "Tell your charge that his lady will await the day when he comes into his garden with great anticipation."[clxxxix]

"But I don't understand!" the young man said. "What of her permission?"

"Her permission?"

"You called her his lady, and yet she has not given her permission!"

"She is mine... it is my permission that is needed, not hers. But, just to reassure you, she and I have talked, and she is prepared, and indeed, eager, to accept my choice for her new lord."

He turned back to me. "Go in peace, my brother, and we will all await with eagerness the return of your charge."

"Thank you. I will go and tell my charge to prepare a place to put this wonderful garden."

"We will miss it," the lord said, wistfully.

I smiled, and looked at the young lords prowling the ramparts, "I imagine that you will have many other gardens soon, and then, if they are fruitful, yet more gardens."

"True, my brother," he said, grinning. "Fare well."

And so I went on my way, musing on the day, which I, too, hoped would not be long, when my charge would come and take possession of this marvelous garden, so tenderly prepared by our common Lord.

XX: A Welcome Phone Call.

Sakal: She called you, from her *honeymoon*?!

Isha: *[Laughing.]* It wasn't a long call, just a quick 'thanks'. She said Andrew had stepped out to get them some food and told her to 'rest'… which she said she couldn't do, so she called me.

Sakal: So, did it sound like she was well on her way to 'doing good and not harm'?

Isha: She admitted that he seemed to be enjoying their honeymoon, and that they were spending an amazingly little amount of time outside.

Sakal: *[Laughs]* Good! Perhaps her father will get his grandchild soon!

Isha: I hope so. Speaking of children…

XXI: After-warning

Reading this book, and reading the Scriptures, the book it is based on, could change your life.

Fathers: it could force you to take up a responsibility that you have, hitherto ignored: that of choosing, or causing to be chosen, a wife for your son, or accepting, yourself, a husband for your daughter. To place your wisdom, your experience, on the block: accepting, forever, the responsibility of giving this good gift to your child.

Sons: Accepting the ideas that Scripture presents for your marriage could cast down the idol that you have constructed for yourself of the girl you will marry. And it will definitely challenge you to take much, much more seriously your own responsibilities toward becoming a Godly husband and father if you become liable to having your father, without warning, suddenly present you with a betrothed wife. Those video games, that 'free time', that you are so addicted to; these will have to go by the wayside; replaced by the responsibilities and joys of spiritual leadership and diapers.

Daughters: You too may have to give up an idol: the idol of choice. Girls never had as much choice as boys, but, perhaps, you have always held on to that last kernel of 'veto'... of being able to send a young boy, not up to your standards, packing. Your idealized marriage (which never was a reality anyway) will have to give way to the reality of a real, live, fallible young man, suddenly bound in covenant to you. And you will find that this fallible young man is exactly who God has prepared for you.

Or perhaps you will need to give up the idea of 'romance'... that a young man will come and 'sweep you off your feet'; the idea of a marriage based on emotion. Instead you need to replace that false and worldly idea with the permanence of covenant: the old idea, the Biblical idea of 'for better or for worse'.

Elders, Pastors: Are you ready to die for the testimony and teachings of the Word of God? Are you ready to face the humiliation that will arise if you stand before your flock and admit that you have gotten it wrong? That the courtship or 'Christian' dating message you have been preaching was, actually, a false front; a compromise of worldly wisdom hiding behind a façade of Christianity?

Titus 2, Proverbs 31, Titus 1... these are wonderful passages. But they, along with Ephesians 5, describe the *results* of marriage, not it's *preconditions*. Titus 2 is specifically written for what the older women are to teach the younger (married) women to *become*. The young, naïve, foolish and disobedient younger woman is taught; taught by God, her husband, and the older women, to: 'love her husband, and to love her children'. It is the married man who is to *become* the man listed in Titus 1; for how can he already be: the husband of one wife, having faithful children not accused of riot or unruly.'

We need to stop putting these obstacles in the way of clear obedience, and be ready to 'let them marry'; to tear down the walls of an unBiblical culture that has prevented hundreds and even thousands of marriages that will result, and result quickly, from an honest application of these principles; that has prevented the hundreds and thousands of children that would have been added to our ranks. We need to be ready to face the mockery of the surrounding communities over what they will no doubt call 'arranged marriages'.

We need to obey God; to demonstrate our love for Him and for our children in our obedience:

1Jn 5:2-5 By this we know that we love the children of God, when we love God, and keep his commandments. For this is the love of God, that we keep his commandments: and his commandments are not grievous. For whatsoever is born of God overcometh the world: and this is the victory that overcometh the world, even our faith. Who is he that overcometh the world, but he that believeth that Jesus is the Son of God.

---

[1] From the Hebrew for 'wise'

[2] From the Hebrew for 'woman' or 'wife'.

[3] From the Greek for 'man'.

[4] From the Hebrew for 'father'.

[5] From the Anglo-Saxon for 'young girl'.

[6] From the French: girl of the earth

[7] From the Greek: Father

[8] From the Hebrew meaning 'daughter'; after the daughter of Jepthah, who bewailed her virginity.

[9] An Americanized version of 'Jezebel'.

[10] French for 'Of the World'

[xi] Prov 19: 3

[xii] Ps 119: 105

[xiii] Rom 7: 18-25

[xiv] I Pet 4: 19

[xv] "I weep for you," the Walrus said. I deeply sympathize. With sobs and tears he sorted out Those of the largest size. Holding his pocket handkerchief Before his streaming eyes. –Lewis Carroll, Alice through the looking glass

[xvi] Matt 22: 37-39

[xvii] II Tim 3: 16-17

xviii Andrew may be thinking of Matt 18: 19 here, but his application is a little off.

xix Prov 12: 15

xx I Cor 6: 20

xxi Job 31: 1

xxii Rom 12: 1

xxiii Matt 19: 12, I Cor 7

xxiv Prov 5: 15-23, I Cor 7: 2-5, Song of Solomon

xxv Prov 3: 5

xxvi Gen 2: 18, Eph 5, I Cor 7, Prov 5, Song of Solomon,

xxvii Ps 127, 128

xxviii Mal 2:14-5

xxix Eph 5:30-32

xxx Indeed, we will not get into it at all in this book. Those who are inclined to think that sex before marriage is acceptable to God are unlikely to follow the reasoning in the rest of this book. I might suggest, 'The Best Things in Life', by Peter Kreeft for a fun answer to this question.

xxxi Prov 5: 23

xxxii I Thes 4: 6

xxxiii billgothard.com/teaching/courtship

xxxiv Prov 1: 20

xxxv "I was desperate! I was so desperate I went to the Word of God!" Kevin Swanson in the film Divided at 33: 59: 00

xxxvi Paul writes: 1Tim 4:1-5 *"Now the Spirit speaketh expressly, that in the latter times some shall depart from the faith, giving heed to seducing spirits, and doctrines of devils; Speaking lies in hypocrisy; having their conscience seared with a hot iron; Forbidding to marry, and commanding to abstain from meats, which God hath created to be received with thanksgiving of them which believe and know the truth. For every creature of God is good, and nothing to be refused, if it be received with thanksgiving: For it is sanctified by the word of God and prayer."* And Col 2:20-24 *"Wherefore if ye be dead with Christ from the rudiments of the world, why, as though living in the world, are ye subject to ordinances, Touch not; taste not; handle not; Which all are to perish with the using;) after the commandments and doctrines of men? Which things have indeed a shew of wisdom in will worship, and humility, and neglecting of the body; not in any honour to the satisfying of the flesh."*

Much of the courtship model seems to be promoting the concept, derived from Gnosticism & Catholicism, that the true, Godly, spiritual married man does not physically 'enjoy' the pleasures of the marriage bed. He has intercourse (when he has it at all) only to obey the commands, "be fruitful & multiply". This stands in stark contrast to the explicit statements commanding physical enjoyment in Prov 5 & the Song of Solomon.

The most severe dichotomy, however, is with the metaphor of Eph 5. Our marriages are supposed to reflect the marriage of Christ and the Church. Thus any failure of intimacy, indeed of rejoicing, between the couple is a rejection of the intimacy, and rejoicing, that is supposed to exist between Christ and the Church. Christ, Himself, continually used metaphors of the bridegroom 'rejoicing in the day of his marriage.'

The path to marriage, then, should include an acknowledgement that it is a good thing, as a goal in itself, to provide a man with a wife (and a wife with a husband) not just so they can be fruitful, not merely to avoid fornication, but so that they can actively and deliberately enjoy the pleasures of the marriage bed.

xxxvii Song 7: 6-9

xxxviii Prov 6: 24-25

xxxix Prov 7:7-9

xl II Tim 3: 16-17, Ps 19, Ps 119, WCF "The whole counsel of God, concerning all things necessary for his own glory, man's salvation, faith, and life, is either expressly set down in Scripture, or by good and necessary consequence may be deduced from Scripture: unto which nothing at any time is to be added..."

xli Acts 15: 20, I Cor 5: 1, I Cor 6: 18, I Cor 7: 2

xlii Job 31: 1

xliii Note: For the purposes of their privacy, we have not actually included a real phone number here. Do not try this at home.

xliv Song 8: 8-10; Eze 16: 7

xlv Prov 5: 18, Isa 54: 6, Mal 2: 14-15, I Cor 7: 36 (stating the girl should be married before she passes 'the flower of her age', which is generally held to mean from between 12 and 20 yo.)

xlvi Eph 6:1-3

xlvii Verses one and two share the same subject: 'children'. Calvin says of verse 1: 1.Children, obey. Why does the apostle use the word obey instead of honor, (167) which has a greater extent of meaning? It is because Obedience is the evidence of that honor which children owe to their parents, and is therefore more earnestly enforced. It is likewise more difficult; for the human mind recoils from the idea of subjection, and with difficulty allows itself to be placed under the control of another. Experience shews how rare this virtue is; for do we find one among a thousand that is obedient to his parents? By a figure of speech, a part is here put for the whole, but it is the most important part, and is necessarily accompanied by all the others.

xlviii This subject is too deep to cover in this book, but Scripture (modern sensibilities aside) is quite clear that the obedience of the son to his father is meant to be lifelong. Christ is quite clear on His relationship with his father, Jeremiah 35 is an interesting case study on the subject but, really, all of Scripture teaches it.

The particular Greek Word in Eph 6:1 (Children obey your parents) is 'teknon' and is used, repeatedly, for individual and groups of adults that are in an authority relationship with someone. For example: 1Jn 3:10 **In this the children of God are manifest, and the children of the devil: whosoever doeth not righteousness is not of God, neither he that loveth not his brother.**

xlix From the Hebrew meaning 'daughter'; after the daughter of Jepthah, who bewailed her virginity.

l "Her Hand in Marriage: Biblical Courtship in the Modern World" by Douglas Wilson, 1997, Cannon Press, Moscow, Idaho

li Pg 52, final paragraph, for example. There he mentions that Abraham, Isaac, and Jacob all married beautiful women. However he gives the impression (being in the middle of a book on courtship) that this was the result of the man 'picking' a beautiful woman. While it might be said that Jacob insisted on Rachel as his second wife in part because of her beauty (in large part because he had already formed a romantic attachment to her) nothing is said of how Abraham got his wife, and in the case of Isaac this is flatly contradicted (as Isaac did not choose Rebecca at all). Abraham's servant picked Rebecca and brought her to Isaac. Yes, she was beautiful, but her beauty played no part in Isaac's choice, since he made no choice.

lii While several Biblical characters play parts in Mr. Wilson's book no character, including Christ, is ever held up as an example of the complete path to marriage because, as Beth points out, they didn't court; and their marriages contradict much of the courting model.

liii ezinearticles.com/?Is-Courtship-an-End-to-Marriage?&id=4143525, ylcf.org/2008/10/giving-your-heart-away/

liv visionarydaughters.com /2010/07/why-am-i-not-married

lv http: //visionarydaughters.com/ 2010/10/greater-expectations

lvi "Returning to our sheep" A French phrase meaning 'coming back to the original subject'.

lvii itwillpass.com/family_dating.shtml

lviii itwillpass.com/family_dating.shtml

lix itwillpass.com/family_dating.shtml, quote from unnamed pastor

lx itwillpass.com/family_dating.shtml

lxi Jer 29: 6, Jdg 21: 7, Ezra 9: 12, Neh 10: 30, I Cor 7: 36-38

lxii Calvin's commentary in his 'Institutes' on the seventh commandment.

lxiii Prov 22: 6, Eph 6: 4

lxiv I Cor 7: 2,9,36

lxv Prov 5: 18, Isa 54: 6, Mal 2: 15

lxvi I Cor 7: 2,9

lxvii Prov 5: 15-23

lxviii Gen 1: 28, Gen 9: 1,7; Gen 35: 11; Lev 26: 9, Ps 127, 128, Mal 2: 15

lxix I Tim 3: 2, Tit 1: 6

lxx Prov 31: 12

lxxi Prov 31: 11

lxxii Gen 24: 33

lxxiii Gen 24: 54-59

lxxiv Calvin on Gen 24:58

lxxv John Gill on Gen 24:58

lxxvi www.ncfic.org/articlemodule /view_category_articles/catid/19/src/@random49598ead4a15d/

lxxvii signonsandiego.com/ uniontrib/ 20060302/news_1c02dating.html

lxxviii In obedience to his father, Jacob proceeded to Ur where he was instructed to marry one of the daughters of Laban. Once there he waited a month before proceeding toward his errand and, even then, fails to mention his father's instructions but instead makes a play for one of those daughters, Rachel, because he 'loved' her (perhaps because she was beautiful and well favored whereas her sister was 'tender eyed'). His love is so great that he volunteers to serve seven years in order to marry her.

When the seven years were up his erstwhile father in law plays him a trick, slipping his oldest daughter, Leah, into the tent instead of the younger and more beautiful Rachel. The next morning Jacob, waking and realizing who lay next to him, faced a choice.

Would he love the wife he was given, the wife he had already spent the night with? Was that not what God required? Is it not written, *'rejoice in the wife of your youth. Let her be as the loving hind and pleasant roe, let her ... satisfy thee at all times; and be thou ravished always with her love'*?

Is that what Jacob did? Did he spend the next week enjoying his new bride, showing his love for her? No, he stormed out of the tent, upset at the trick that had been played on him. But, except for his premarital mental commitment, what trick had been played? He had been commanded by his father to take a wife of the daughters of Laban, and he had a wife of the daughters of Laban. And we know, from later in the story, that she was a fertile wife. He came out with no complaints about her behavior on the wedding night. No, he was disappointed because he had set his heart on one particular woman, and was given another. He had, in modern parlance, 'fallen in love' and, as a result, behaved abominably toward the wife of his youth, going so far in his misbehavior that God Himself accuses him of hating his wife.

Compare this with the example of his father Isaac.

Isaac saw nothing of his wife, knew nothing of his wife, before he took her into his tent and 'knew' her physically. And, without a heart set on another, he loved his wife.

lxxix *"And [Shechem's] soul clave unto Dinah the daughter of Jacob, and he loved the damsel, and spake kindly unto the damsel."* Unfortunately this comes after the previous verse which states he, *"saw her, he took her, and lay with her, and defiled her."* Only once he had done these two things (raped her and 'loved' her) did he *"[speak] unto his father Hamor, saying, Get me this damsel to wife."*

And then her brothers, mightily offended, tricked and slew Shekem and all the men of his town.

lxxx David with Michal and Bathsheba.

lxxxi I Sam 18:21

lxxxii II Sam 11:2 and following.

lxxxiii II Sam 13

lxxxiv Jud 14,15

lxxxv Gen 2: 18

lxxxvi I Cor 7:2

lxxxvii Indeed, Calvin writes: "Nor is it merely fornicators that he restrains, but those also who are defiled in the sight of God by inward lust" and the Geneva commentary: "So to burn with lust, that either the will yields to the temptation, or else we cannot call upon God with a peaceful conscience."

lxxxviii *"Nevertheless, to avoid fornication, let every man have his own wife, and every woman her own husband."*

lxxxix I Cor 7:8, Matt 19:10-12

xc John Calvin

xci John Gill, commentary on I Cor 7: 9

xcii Matthew Henry on I Cor 7:2

xciii Matthew Henry on I Cor 7:9

xciv sermonaudio.com/sermoninfo.asp ?SID=6230484014

xcv Prov 5: 15-23

xcvi Sakal would have issues with the concept of a 'youth pastor' anyway. www.ncfic.org/confession

xcvii Prov was written as instructions to young men, and often speaks of sexual issues. The Song is also in Scripture, and we are never called to give our young men an expurgurated version of the Scriptures.

xcviii Her Hand in Marriage, pg 53

xcix Her Hand in Marriage, pg 16

c Jer 17: 9

ci I Cor 7:2,0; Prov 5:15-23

cii Matt 9: 12-13, Jam 2: 15-16, I Cor 7: 9

ciii Scott Brown, in the film Divided by the brothers O'Clerk, at approx 50 minutes.

civ Ibid, approx 30 mins into the film.

cv Paul Washer. Ibid. Approx 49 mins.

cvi Matt 11: 30

cvii Eph 5:25, "Husbands love your wives' is a command, not a statement of feelings.

cviii worldspirituality.org/christian-courtship.html

cix worldspirituality.org/christian-courtship.html

cx worldspirituality.org/christian-courtship.html

cxi I Cor 7: 39

cxii II Cor 6: 14

cxiii A later verse in the passage reads: *"Wherefore come out from among them, and be ye separate, saith the Lord, and touch not the unclean thing; and I will receive you,"* This, if applied to marriage, would contradict I Cor 7: 12-14 *"But to the rest speak I, not the Lord: If any brother hath a wife that believeth not, and she be pleased to dwell with him, let him not put her away. And the woman which hath an husband that believeth not, and if he be pleased to dwell with her, let her not leave him. For the unbelieving husband is sanctified by the wife, and the unbelieving wife is sanctified by the husband: else were your children unclean; but now are they holy."*

cxiv Gen 26: 34

cxv I Sam 18: 25

cxvi Josh 15: 17

cxvii Moses, Joseph, Joash, Ishmael…

cxviii John 15: 16

cxix John 17: 2

cxx Ezra 10

cxxi Esther 2:8

cxxii Gen 41: 45

cxxiii Exod2: 21

cxxiv Hosea 1: 2

cxxv Deu 25:5

cxxvi Gen 2: 18

cxxvii Prov 18: 22

cxxviii Gen 2: 18

cxxix Prov 31:10-31, Prov 18:22, Titus 2:5, Ps 127,128

cxxx Pro 27: 6

cxxxi Gen 2: 18

cxxxii Not an issue that we address in this book, but Ps 127 and other passages clearly list children, many children, as a blessing God bestows on a man (and his wife).

cxxxiii Matt19:12

cxxxiv Prov 18:22: Nowhere in Scripture do we find anything like the modern theory about 'bad matches'. Instead we see husbands and wives responsible for their own actions within every marriage. The example of Christ shows how a husband should behave with a 'bad' wife.

cxxxv Vodie Baucham, on the CD "The Four P's".

cxxxvi Prov 5: 18-19

cxxxvii Gen 2: 22

cxxxviii Gen 24

cxxxix Gen 24: 50b-51

cxl Gen 29

cxli II Tim 3: 16-17

cxlii Ruth 3: 1-5

cxliii Deu 25: 5-6

cxliv Ruth 1: 16

cxlv Josh 15: 17

cxlvi I Sam 18: 27

cxlvii See the story about Mark and Rachel in myweb.tiscali.co.uk/ largerhope/ Courtship %20&%20Betrothal% 20Essays/B.H.S.htm

cxlviii Deut 22: 28-9; Exod22: 16-17

cxlix I Cor 7: 9

cl www.worldspirituality.org/christian-courtship.html

cli Gen 2: 18

clii Prov 31: 10-31

cliii I Tim 5:2

cliv visionarydaughters.com /2010/07/why-am-i-not-married

clv The Biblical name for the uniting in sexual intercourse is, alternately, 'knew here', 'come together', or 'take' the wife. See, for example, Gen 24: 67

clvi John 14: 1-3

clvii Prov 24: 27

clviii several points needed to be noted about Prov 24:7:

a) The verse says nothing about marriage.

b) The verse speaks of 'a field', which would have been, under Jewish law, something that one would have gotten either when purchased in addition to one's own land, or when one's father died... neither one a young man's occupation. So the person involved here probably already has a wife, and children, who are probably engaged in helping him put the field in order before they build their new house on their new land.

c) Putting the interpretation of marriage to this verse puts the young wife as a 'liability', or a 'luxury'; something which drains rather than increases the young man's ability to produce, to prepare his field. This is not how Scripture speaks of a wife. Instead it sees the wife as someone who is productive in the young man's endeavors. Indeed, according to Prov 31, it might have been the wife herself who bought the field!

d) The actual words of the verse admit of an obvious meaning that fits perfectly into much else that Prov says; contrasting the wise man and the fool. A man who buys a field and, before getting the land in shape and planting a crop, instead builds the house (instead of living in a tent, as would be natural) is a fool. The contrary man, who prepares the field to be productive before working on the house, is a wise man.

clix I Cor 14:8

clx II Tim 3:15-17

clxi James 2:14-17

clxii I Tim 4:3

clxiii Eg: generationsof.blogspot.com /2007/06/establishing-multi-generational-vision.html

clxiv See: www.visionforum.com /browse/product/?productid=52842

clxv This is a direct quote from Jer 29:6 but is also inferred from many other passages including I Cor 7.

clxvi See I Cor 7:36, '*if she pass the flower of her age*.' Many of our daughters are getting older and older, and have long passed 'the flower of their age' and almost passed their fertility, and they still aren't married.

clxvii Song 4:12

clxviii Song 4:12

clxix Song 8:9

clxx Song 4:15; Prov 5:15-18

clxxi Prov 5:15-18

clxxii Song 4:13;

clxxiii Song 6:2,3; Song 2:16; Song 5:13; Song 7:2;

clxxiv Song 4:3; Song 4;13;

clxxv Song 7:7-8;

clxxvi Song 6:11

clxxvii Song 4;10-16; Song 6:2; Song 8:14

clxxviii Song 8:8-9; Gen 34

clxxix Deu 22:21; Song 8:9

clxxx Gen 24:33

clxxxi I Cor 7:2,9

clxxxii Gen 29:15

clxxxiii Num 30:3-5

clxxxiv Deu 22:21; Song 8:8-9

clxxxv Num 30:3-5

clxxxvi I Cor 7:2

clxxxvii I Cor 7:1-9

clxxxviii Exod 22:17; Prov 31: 10

clxxxix Rom 8:23-25